Study Guide for

Spielvogel's

Western Civilization
A Brief History

Volume II: Since 1500
Second Edition

James T. Baker
Western Kentucky University

WADSWORTH

THOMSON LEARNING

Australia • Canada • Mexico • Singapore • Spain • United Kingdom • United States

Printed in Canada
1 2 3 4 5 6 7 05 04 03 02 01

ISBN 0-534-58713-5

For more information, contact
Wadsworth/Thomson Learning
10 Davis Drive
Belmont, CA 94002-3098
USA

For more information about our products, contact us:
Thomson Learning Academic Resource Center
1-800-423-0563
http://www.wadsworth.com

International Headquarters
Thomson Learning
International Division
290 Harbor Drive, 2nd Floor
Stamford, CT 06902-7477
USA

UK/Europe/Middle East/South Africa
Thomson Learning
Berkshire House
168-173 High Holborn
London WC1V 7AA
United Kingdom

Asia
Thomson Learning
60 Albert Complex, #15-01
Singapore 189969

Canada
Nelson Thomson Learning
1120 Birchmount Road
Toronto, Ontario M1K 5G4
Canada

CONTENTS

PREFACE

This study guide was prepared to accompany the text *Western Civilization: A Brief History* by Jackson J. Spielvogel. The first volume, which includes Chapters 1-16, can be used in conjunction with *Volume I: to 1715*. The second volume, which includes Chapters 12-29, can be used in conjunction with *Volume II: Since 1500*.

The guide contains seven types of exercises for each of the chapters:

a. Words to identify—important names, places, ideas, and works of literature, art, and music to know and understand.
b. Words to match with their definitions—important terms to be matched with their meanings, a second form of identification.
c. Multiple-choice questions—a way of testing factual and conceptual learning.
d. Sentences to complete—spaces are provided to complete an interpretive statement with specific words and phrases.
e. Chronological arrangement—for each chapter, a set of seven events to place in chronological order and give their dates.
f. Questions for critical thought—questions that ask you to recall and relate important concepts and prepare for essay examinations.
g. Analysis of primary source documents—questions that ask you to apply the information found in documents, from the time period studied, that are presented in the boxes of each chapter.

Answers to exercises b, c, d, and e are found at the end of the guide.

In addition, at the end of certain chapters, there are map exercises to test your knowledge of geography important to the various historical periods. You may check your completed maps with the appropriate ones in the text.

You will probably be asked to write essays during your examinations. Essays not only test your knowledge of the facts, but your ability to interpret and apply them. Pay particular attention to the questions asked after the topics presented in the "Questions for Critical Thought" section of each chapter. These questions will help you organize your essay answers. In addition, the suggestions below on how to write essays will both teach you and help you make high marks:

a. Read the entire question, and be sure that you understand exactly what is being asked and that you have considered all parts of it. Address yourself only to the question that is asked, but address yourself to every section of that question.

b. Make an outline before you begin to write the essay. Jot down, in as few words as possible, the major points you want to make, and the most important persons, places, and ideas you want to include. Glance back at your outline as you write so that you will not stay too long on one point or omit another.

c. Try to make one major point in your essay, with all of the others subordinate to it. This is your thesis. State it at the beginning, refer back to it at various appropriate times, and restate it briefly at the end. This will keep you focused on a unifying theme.

d. Write for an imaginary reader (who will be your teacher or an assistant, but you may not know exactly who it will be) who is intelligent, but does not necessarily know the information you are relating. This way you will not fail to provide all information necessary to explain yourself, but you will also not insult your reader.

e. Be careful to spell correctly and to use good grammar. A history course is not an English course, and graders may or may not "count off" for poor spelling and grammar; however all graders are impressed either positively or negatively by the care with which you write. While you may not see a specific comment about such matters on your essay, you may be sure that they have affected your final grade.

f. View writing an essay in a positive light. It should and can be an exercise in which the facts you have learned take focus and shape and make more sense than ever before. If done correctly, an essay can be the truest learning experience you can have, and the most certain measure of your achievement.

I hope that this booklet adds to your enjoyment of the study of *Western Civilization*, increases your understanding of the material contained in it, and leads to a good grade in your course.

James T. Baker
Western Kentucky University

CHAPTER

12 RECOVERY AND REBIRTH: THE AGE OF THE RENAISSANCE

Chapter Outline:

I.   Meaning and Characteristics of the Italian Renaissance
    A.   An Urban Society
    B.   An Age of Recovery
    C.   A Rebirth of Classical Culture
    D.   The Individual

II.   The Making of Renaissance Society
    A.   Economic Recovery
        1.   The Hanseatic League
        2.   Manufacturing and Banking
    B.   Social Changes
        1.   Domination of the Nobility
        2.   Courtly Society and Castiglione's *Courtier*
        3.   Peasants and Townspeople
        4.   The Family: Leon Battista Alberbti

III. The Italian States in the Renaissance
    A.   The Five Major States: Milan, Venice, Florence, the Papal States, and Naples
    B.   The Examples of Federigo da Montefeltro and Isabella d'Este
    C.   Machiavelli and the New Statecraft

IV.   The Intellectual Renaissance in Italy
    A.   Humanism
        1.   Petrarch
        2.   Leonardo Bruni
    B.   Humanism and Philosophy
        1.   Ficino and the Platonic Academy
        2.   Pico della Mirandola

C.   Education: Vittorino da Feltre and "Liberal Studies"
D.   The Impact of Printing
    1.   Johannes Gutenberg
    2.   Scholarly Research

V.   The Artistic Renaissance
    A.   The Early Renaissance
        1.   Masaccio
        2.   Donatello
        3.   Brunelleschi
    B.   The High Renaissance
        1.   Leonardo da Vinci
        2.   Raphael
        3.   Michelangelo
    C.   The Northern Artistic Renaissance
        1.   Jan Van Eyck
        2.   Albrecht Dürer

VI.   The European State in the Renaissance
    A.   Louis XI and France
    B.   Henry VII and England
    C.   Ferdinand, Isabella, and Spain
    D.   Central Europe: The Holy Roman Empire
    E.   The Struggle for Strong Monarchy in Eastern Europe
    F.   The Ottoman Turks and the End of the Byzantine Empire

VII.   The Church in the Renaissance
    A.   The Problems of Heresy and Reform
        1.   John Hus
        2.   Reform Decrees
    B.   The Renaissance Papacy
        1.   Sixtus IV
        2.   Alexander VI
        3.   Julius II
        4.   Leo X

Chapter Summary:

The Age of the Renaissance is one of our most recognized eras, populated with artists and writers of great genius, vivid imagination, and amazing skill. Yet the violence of its rising political leaders and daring of its financiers made it, as one historian has said, an age characterized by "the mixed scent of blood and roses."

The strong economic recovery of the day, prefiguring the modern world, created a refined courtly society that supported the arts but planted seeds of envy in the hearts of peasants and city laborers who did not share the wealth. Strong Italian merchants and European kings gained enormous power. Writers and artists, widely honored for their work, served at the pleasure and taste of wealthy patrons. Renaissance popes, freeing themselves from the fourteenth century's chaos, used their office to enrich themselves and their families. Heresy loomed, and intellectuals called for reform.

Still the roll call of personalities—the writers Castiglione, Machiavelli, Ficino, and Pico and the artists Leonardo, Michelangelo, Raphael—confirms that the Renaissance was indeed an age of genius and achievement, one of the high points in Western civilization.

The dominant intellectual movement of the age was humanism. Relying on the "liberal arts" curriculum of the High Middle Ages, humanists recovered and taught from classical Greek and Roman texts, based their literary, philosophical, and artistic work on classical models, and proclaimed with the ancients that "man is the measure of all things."

Identify:

1.   Jacob Burckhardt   [p. 236] *Swiss historian + art critic created the modern concept of the renaissance in his celebrated work Civilization of the Ren. pub in 1860*

2.   Isabella d'Este   [p. 243] *Daughter of the Duke of Ferrara + who married the Marquis of Mantua - known for intellectual political wisdom "first lady of the world" - attracted artists + intellectuals to the Mantua court + amassed one of the finest libraries*

3.   Machiavelli   [pp. 243-244] *in one of Italy, author of the "realistic" treatise, The Prince - a prince's attitude toward power must be based on understanding of human nature*

4.   Petrarch   [p. 245] *called the father of human renaissance humanism, Cicero.*

5.   Pico della Mirandola   [p. 246-247] *- Oration of the Dignity of Man. - avid interest in Hermetic philosophy*

6.   Johannes Gutenberg   [p. 247] *- Gutenberg's Bible was the first true book in the west produced w movable type*

7.   Masaccio   [p. 248] *frescoes by Masaccio's in the Brancacci chapel in Florentine = first masterpiece of early Renaissance art.*

Tribute money

8.   Donatello   [p. 249] *David - simplicity + strength that reflected the dignity of humanity.*

9.   Brunelleschi   [p. 249] *- friend of Donatello's who accompanied to Rome - classical columns - designed the church of San Lorenzo - rounded arch*

10.   Louis XI   [p. 253] *French King Spider because of his wily + devious ways*

11.   Henry VII   [p. 253] *First Tudor King*

12. John Hus [p. 256] *chancellor of the university of Prague, urged the Renaissance to ... christianized of the humanities, attacked the corruption of the clergy, attacked the excessive power of the papacy within the catholic church.*

13. Julius II [p. 256] *Renaissance pope most involved in war + politics, "warrior pope"*

14. Leo X [p. 257] *Julius' successor - a patron of renaissance culture - medici pope who commissioned Raphael to paint frescoes in the Vatican*

Match the following words with their definitions:

1. Castiglione

2. Machiavelli

3. Leonardo Bruni

4. Marsilio Ficino

5. Pico della Mirandola

6. Michelangelo

7. Louis XI

8. Henry VII

9. Julius II

10. Leo X

A. Florentine who founded the Platonic Academy

B. artist whose work reflects his devotion to neoplatonic philosophy

C. first Tudor King

D. author of the Renaissance book on etiquette, *The Courtier*

E. warrior pope who decided to rebuild Saint Peter's Church

F. scholar who made Cicero the pattern for Renaissance literary style

G. Medici pope who commissioned Raphael to paint frescoes in the Vatican

H. humanist who wrote the "Oration on the Dignity of Man"

I. author of the "realistic" political treatise *The Prince*

J. "Spider King" known for his wily administration

Multiple Choice:

1. Economic developments in the Renaissance included

   a. the concentration of wealth in fewer hands.
   b. increased employment as wool gave way to luxury goods.
   c. an economic boom that rivaled the Middle Ages.
   d. new trade opened by the Ottoman Turks.

2.   Castiglione's *Courtier*

    a.   rejected the idea of a classical education.
    b.   praised the courtly life.
    c.   advocated Hedonism.
    d.   disapproved of the political life.

3.   Banquets in the Renaissance

    a.   reflected the simplicity of life idealized in the courtly poetry.
    b.   were never held on Holy Days or after weddings.
    c.   were used to demonstrate wealth and power.
    d.   were banned by the papacy.

4.   Towns and cities of the fifteenth century had populations

    a.   in which there was little social classification.
    b.   of various religious persuasions.
    c.   relatively free of disease and criminal activity.
    d.   widely separated socially and economically.

5.   In the Renaissance family
    a.   women managed all domestic finances.
    b.   marriages were arranged by parents.
    c.   children became adults upon reaching their eighteenth birthday.
    d.   dowries ceased to play a significant role in marriage arrangements.

6.   Machiavelli's *Prince* paved the way for

    a.   an Italian democratic movement.
    b.   higher moral standards for political figures.
    c.   the modern secular concept of power politics.
    d.   all of the above

7.   Pico della Mirandola's *Oration on the Dignity of Man* stated that humans

    a.   are fallen creatures but can regain their place by humiliating themselves before God.
    b.   are nothing more than amoral beasts.
    c.   are divine and destined for eternal glory.
    d.   can choose to be either earthly or spiritual creatures.

8. Renaissance humanists taught that "liberal studies"

    a. enable men to reach their full potential.
    b. should be taught only by laymen.
    c. are incompatible with a strong emphasis on physical training.
    d. are best taught in coeducational classes.

9. Italian artists of the fifteenth century began to

    a. ignore nature and paint from the inner light.
    b. emphasize realism and perspective.
    c. return to the styles of the twelfth century artists.
    d. ignore the study of anatomy.

10. Catholicism in the fifteenth century saw

    a. popes leading crusades for higher moral standards for kings.
    b. the Conciliar Movement significantly weaken the papacy.
    c. John Hus burned at the stake as a heretic.
    d. papal condemnation of nudity in the visual arts.

Complete the following sentences:

1. The Italian city of Florence grew to preeminence due to the rise of the _Medici_ family, whose _dynasty_ had branches in several cities and whose mines produced _alum_.

2. Castiglione, in his *Book of the _Courtier_*, outlined the ideal character of and conduct for the Renaissance _courtier_, whose primary aim, he said, should be to serve his _prince_.

3. Isabella d'Este, educated at the court of _Ferrara_, attracted humanists to her husband's court at _Mantua_, where she built a grand _library_.

4. Having lost his position as a Florentine _diplomat_, Machiavelli turned his mind to political theory and wrote a political treatise called _The Prince_. In it he denied that politics should be restricted by any _moral?_ concerns.

5. Considered the Father of Renaissance humanism, _Petrarch_ said prose should be patterned after _Cicero_ and poetry after _Virgil_.

6.   The High Renaissance was dominated by three artistic geniuses. Oldest to youngest, they were: _Leonardo_ , _Michelangelo_ , and _Raphael_ .

7.   In his painting _The_ _Last_ _Supper_ , done in Milan, Leonardo da Vinci sought to reveal the _inner_ _life_ of his figures.

8.   In his famous _School_ _of_ _Athens_ , Raphael illustrated the Renaissance ideals of _Plato_ , _Aristotle_ , and _Pythagoras_ .

9.   On the Sistine ceiling, Michelangelo's _____ figures were intended to reflect _____ _____ .

10.   Renaissance popes had unsavory reputations, particularly the warrior-pope _Julius_ _II_ , the pope who made five of his nephews cardinals, _Sixtus_ _IV_ , and the pope who was infamous for his debauchery, _Alexander_ _VI_ .

Place the following in chronological order and give dates:

1.   Marriage of Ferdinand and Isabella   1.

2.   First Medici reaches papal throne as Leo X   2.

3.   End of the Great Schism   3.

4.   Cosimo dé Medici takes power in Florence   4.

5.   Expulsion of the Spanish Jews   5.

6.   First Gutenberg Bible printed   6.

7.   Battle of Bosworth Field   7.

Questions for Critical Thought: In each essay fully explore the topic by answering the questions that follow it.

1.   The Life of the Renaissance. What was the Renaissance like socially as reflected in Castiglione's *Courtier*? What was it like politically as reflected in Machiavelli's *Prince*? What was it like intellectually as reflected in the works of Bruni and Pico?

2.   Renaissance Humanism. What was the philosophical notion behind the movement known as humanism? How did this philosophy affect literature, philosophy, education, and the visual arts in the Renaissance?

3.   The Renaissance in Northern Europe. Why and how did Renaissance ideas and ideals move from Italy into other parts of Europe? Who were its representatives in the North? How was the Northern Renaissance like and unlike its Southern counterpart? What effect did it have on Northern thought and society?

4.   The Renaissance Papacy. What theological and political problems did popes during the Renaissance period face? What kind of person became pope at this time? How did each one deal with the problems of the time? What did each accomplish?

Analysis of Primary Source Documents:

1.   What conclusions can be drawn about the wealthy Renaissance man's diet and probable health by perusing the menu from one of Pope Pius V's banquets? Do you consider it proper for a pope and his guests to enjoy such food? Why or why not?

2.   According to the letters of Alessandra Strozzi, what characteristics and advantages did a Renaissance family look for when searching out a wife for one of its sons? What kind of marriage would likely result from such plotting?

3.   What was Machiavelli's advice to a prince who wanted to gain and hold power? Do you feel that he is completely serious, or is he in any way being sarcastic?

4.   What was the Renaissance image of man? Use Pico della Mirandola's *Oration* to demonstrate what humanists believed man's nature and potential to be.

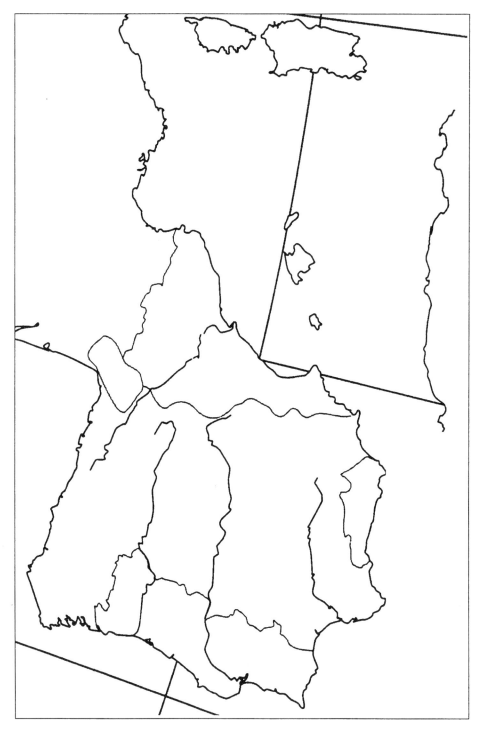

Map Exercise 7

Map Exercise 7:   The Iberian Peninsula in 1479

Using various colors of pencil, shade and label the following:

1.   Aragon
2.   Castile
3.   France
4.   Holy Roman Empire
5.   Papal States

Pinpoint and label the following:

1.   Barcelona
2.   Florence
3.   Madrid
4.   Mainz
5.   Naples
6.   Paris
7.   Rome
8.   Venice

13 THE AGE OF REFORMATION

Chapter Outline:

I.   Prelude to Reformation
    A.   Christian (Northern Renaissance) Humanism
        1.   Reform through Education
        2.   Erasmus and *The Praise of Folly*
    B.   Church and Religion on the Eve of the Reformation
        1.   Abuses of the Clergy
        2.   Popular Religion: Thomas à Kempis

II. Martin Luther and the Reformation in Germany
    A.   The Early Luther
        1.   The Monastic Life
        2.   Justification by Grace through Faith
        3.   Attack on the Sale of Indulgences: The Ninety-Five Theses
        4.   Trial at Worms
    B.   The Development of Lutheranism
        1.   An Urban Phenomenon
        2.   Support for Authority against the Peasants
        3.   The Union of Church and State: National Churches
    C.   Germany and the Reformation: Religion and Politics
        1.   Emperor Charles V's Attempt to Preserve Christian Unity
        2.   The Peace of Augsburg: The Success of Lutheranism

III. The Spread of the Protestant Reformation
    A.   Ulrich Zwingli in Switzerland
    B.   The Radical Reformation: The Anabaptists
        1.   The Church as a Body of Believers
        2.   Separation of Church and State
        3.   Menno Simons and the Mennonites

C.   The Reformation in England
    1.   Henry VIII's Divorce and Separation from Rome
    2.   Edward VI and a More Protestant Church
    3.   Mary I's Attempt to Restore Catholicism
D.   John Calvin and Calvinism
    1.   *Institutes of the Christian Religion*
    2.   The Doctrine of Predestination
    3.   Calvin's Geneva and the Spread of Calvinism

IV.   The Social Impact of the Reformation
    A.   The Effect on Families
    B.   Religious Practices and Popular Culture

V.   The Catholic Reformation
    A.   Loyola and the Jesuits
    B.   A Revived Papacy
        1.   Paul III and the Council of Trent
        2.   Paul IV and the Index
    C.   The Council of Trent

Chapter Summary:

The great religious earthquake called the Reformation, which split the church into two and then into a dozen parts, was caused by a variety of social and economic developments. Still, it depended upon the Renaissance humanism of its day for an intellectual rationale. Christian humanists, particularly in the north of Europe, led the movement to reform and purify the Catholic Church, even though some such as Erasmus in the end refused to be Protestants; and it was their writings that gave the Reformation its direction.

The Reformation began with Martin Luther's criticism of the sale of indulgences and his subsequent excommunication. It spread from Germany to Switzerland through the work of John Calvin and Ulrich Zwingli and to Scotland and Holland through the work of Calvin's disciples. Although in England the break with the Catholic Church came because Henry VIII wanted a divorce, the English Reformation grew more radical after Henry's death. Christendom fragmented.

While northern Europe, with the notable exceptions of France, Poland, and Ireland, left the Catholic faith, the southern nations of Italy, Spain, and Portugal, as well as France and Austria, remained firmly Catholic. The Council of Trent, called too late to stop the permanent division, confirmed the Catholic teachings of the Middle Ages while implementing many of the reforms of practice advocated by Luther and Calvin. The Age of Reformation left all of the churches stronger in conviction, yet at war with each other over authority.

After the tumultuous sixteenth century, Western civilization was never again a religious unity. For better or worse, it entered the modern world divided and at odds with itself over the truth and will of God.

Identify:

1. Pluralism [p. 262]

   the holding of multiple church offices. - church officeholders ignored their duties thru underlings who often had even less interest in the j do.

2. Thomas à Kempis [p. 263]

   The Imitation of Christ ... how religiously we have lived.

3. Indulgences [p. 264]

   People were guaranteeing their eternal damnation by relying on these pieces of paper to assure themselves of salvation.

4. Johann Tetzel [p. 264]

   Dominican selling indulgences "As soon as the coin in the coffer [money box] rings, the soul from purgatory springs."

5. Edict of Worms [pp. 265-266]

   By the Edict of Worms, Luther was made an outlaw within the empire.

   Summoned to appear before the imperial diet of Reichstag of the Holy Roman Empire in Worms.

6. Peace of Augsburg [p. 268]

   the end to religious warfare in Germany - divisions of Christianity acknowledged - Lutheranism granted equal standing w/ Catholicism - each german ruler to to its determine the religion of its subjects.

7. Anabaptists [pp. 270-271]

   - radicals advocated adult baptism + believed that the true christian should not actively participate in a the government by the secular state.

8. Catherine of Aragon [p. 271]

   Henry VIII's first wife, who failed to produce a male heir. He wanted a divorce.

9. Predestination [p. 272]

   Calvin— God had predestined some people to be saved (the elect) + others to be damned (reprobate).

10. Society of Jesus [pp. 274-276]

    The Jesuits — founded by a Spanish nobleman Ignatius of Loyola

11. The Index [p. 276]

    The Index of Forbidden books, a list of books that catholics were not allowed to read, with the first pope of the Catholic Counter-Reformation Paul IV

12. Council of Trent [pp. 276-278]

    - met on the border between Germany + Italy to come to a compromise, by encouraging Protestants to return to the church.

① established highly disciplined schools

② propagation of the Catholic faith among non-christians.

③ determined to carry the catholic banner and fight Protestantism.

Match the following words with their definitions:

1.	Erasmus	A.	Dominican seller of indulgences
2.	Thomas à Kempis	B.	Henry VIII's second wife
3.	Johann Tetzel	C.	Dutch Anabaptist who practiced pacifism
4.	Ulrich Zwingli	D.	humanist whose writings inspired reformist thought, *then came Luther.*
5.	Menno Simons	E.	favored by predestination
6.	Anne Boleyn	F.	author of *The Imitation of Christ*
7.	Thomas Cranmer	G.	founder of the Society of Jesus
8.	Mary Tudor	H.	Archbishop of Canterbury who granted Henry VIII's divorce
9.	The Elect	I.	tried to restore England to the Catholic faith
10.	Ignatius Loyola	J.	leader of the Swiss Reformed Church movement

Multiple Choice:

1. Erasmus hoped to reform Christianity through all of the following *except*

   a. spreading the radical reform ideas of Luther.
   b. satirizing the external habits of the church.
   c. translating the Bible and early church fathers.
   d. teaching the "philosophy of Christ" as a guide for daily life.

2. Thomas à Kempis argued that in the day of judgement men will be examined through their
   a. valor as Christian soldiers in the field.   *... how religiously we have lived.*
   b. public confessions of faith.
   c. financial contributions to spiritual missions.
   d. personal piety.

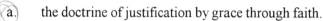

3. Martin Luther's early life was characterized by

   a. failure to follow the daily routine of monastic life.
   b. an obsession with his own sinfulness.
   c. love for the study of law.
   d. rejection of the Bible as the Word of God.

4. Luther finally concluded that one is "saved" by

   a. the doctrine of justification by grace through faith.
   b. doing good works aimed at achieving universal brotherhood.
   c. following the Rule of the Augustinian Order throughout his life.
   d. taking the sacraments every day.

5. The Peasants' War of 1524-1525

   a. was led by Lutheran theologian Philipp Melanchthon.
   b. helped spread Lutheranism throughout Europe.
   c. was praised by Luther for bringing down the Catholic Church.
   d. was primarily a revolt against local lords.

6. The Swiss reformer Ulrich Zwingli tried in vain to

   a. take away Charles V's lands in Germany.
   b. restore Queen Mary to the English throne.
   c. make a pact of religious union with the Lutherans.
   d. keep Catholic practices in his new church.

7. The reign of England's Queen Mary was noted for

   a. her failure to restore Catholicism.
   b. constant warfare with her Spanish territories.
   c. an end to the English Reformation.
   d. an Act of Supremacy in 1534.

8.   Which of the following statements best applies to John Calvin's reform movement?

   a.   Its rejection of Luther's doctrine of "justification by faith alone" made it "Catholic" in attitude.
   b.   Its doctrine of Predestination made it essentially a passive faith.
   c.   Its belief that men must "obey God rather than man" made Calvinism a dynamic and activist faith.
   d.   Its conviction that God watches man's personal deeds kept it from interfering in people's private lives.

9.   The Reformation changed the family in Protestant societies by

   a.   transforming the role of women by opening public careers to them.
   b.   restricting the role of women to those of wife and mother.
   c.   praising celibacy over marriage.
   d.   encouraging women to enter the ministry.

10.   Following the Council of Trent, the Catholic Church

   a.   possessed a clear body of doctrine under a supreme pontiff.
   b.   declared always that it was the only institution that could interpret scripture.
   c.   reaffirmed continually the doctrines of Purgatory and the Virgin Birth of Christ.
   d.   all of the above

Complete the following sentences:

1.   In his book, *The Praise of* ___Folly___, Erasmus satirized ___practices___ in his society and clerical ___corruption___ in his church.

2.   Martin Luther, an ___Augustinian___ monk, in his ___Ninety-five___ Theses openly condemned the sale of ___indulgences___.

3.   In the greatest social upheaval of his lifetime, the Peasants War, Luther sided with _____ against the _____, and this made him dependent upon _____ _____ for the defense of his movement.
   German   State

4.   Ulrich Zwingli ultimately failed in his attempt to unite the reformed churches of ___Germany___ and ___Switzerland___ when they could not agree on their interpretations of the ___Lord's___ ___Supper___.

5.   Anabaptists baptized only _adults_, considered each Christian a _priest_, and encouraged each church to pick its own _ministers_.

6.   Thomas Cranmer helped Henry VIII divorce Queen _Catherine_ and marry _Anne Boleyn_, then helped move England toward Protestantism under Henry's heir, _Queen Mary_.

7.   John Calvin's emphasis in his great book, _Institutes_ *of the Christian Religion*, on the absolute _Sovereignty_ of God made the doctrine of _predestination_ central to his creed.

8.   Protestantism took away women's religious profession, the life of a nun, and said they must be only _wives_ and _mothers_, this being punishment for the sin of _Eve_.

9.   The Society of Jesus, founded by _Ignatius_ of _Loyola_, took on the character of his profession and made its members _soldiers_ of God, followers of the Rule he set down in his book *The* _Spiritual Exercises_.

10.   Pope Paul III tried to solve the Protestant revolt by calling a _____ to meet at _Trent_ in 1545. He also revived the Holy Office, the _____ _____, to search out doctrinal errors among Catholics.

Place the following in chronological order and give dates:

1.   Society of Jesus recognized   1.

2.   English Act of Supremacy   2.

3.   Council of Trent convenes   3.

4.   Peace of Augsburg   4.

5.   Death of Mary I of England   5.

6.   Calvin's *Institutes* published   6.

7.   Luther excommunicated   7.

Questions for Critical Thought: In each essay fully explore the topic by answering the questions that follow it.

1.   The Lutheran Revolt. What conditions in the Church of the early sixteenth century made a revolt both possible and probable? What role did Erasmus play in the Lutheran explosion? What were Luther's motivations for leading this religious uprising? How did his personality affect the direction it took?

2.   Protestantism on the Continent. What were Calvin's role in and contribution to the Reformation? What were Zwingli's role and contribution? What did the Anabaptists add to the mix? Generally speaking, what was European Protestantism?

3.   The English Reformation. What caused the Reformation in England? How did it differ, both in causation and direction, from the Reformation on the continent? What were the results, both short and long term, of the English departure from the Catholic faith?

4.   The Catholic Reformation. What leaders brought about this reform, what did they want to do, and how well did they accomplish their goals? What happened at the Council of Trent that made Catholicism truly different from Protestantism? How did the Catholic Reformation shape the Church of the modern era?

Analysis of Primary Source Documents:

1.   How and why did Martin Luther's classroom exercise, The Ninety-Five Theses, cause such a sensation and have such an impact on his society and times?

2.   Using the Marburg Colloquy as your guide, draw as many conclusions as you can about Luther's personality, mind, and public manner.

3.   If Catherine Zell is typical of the Anabaptist faith, what new themes did this movement bring to Christianity? To what extent were these themes the natural consequences of Luther's doctrinal innovations?

4.   If one followed Loyola's formula for correct Christian thinking, what would a Christian believe? How would a Christian act? What would a Christian seek to accomplish?

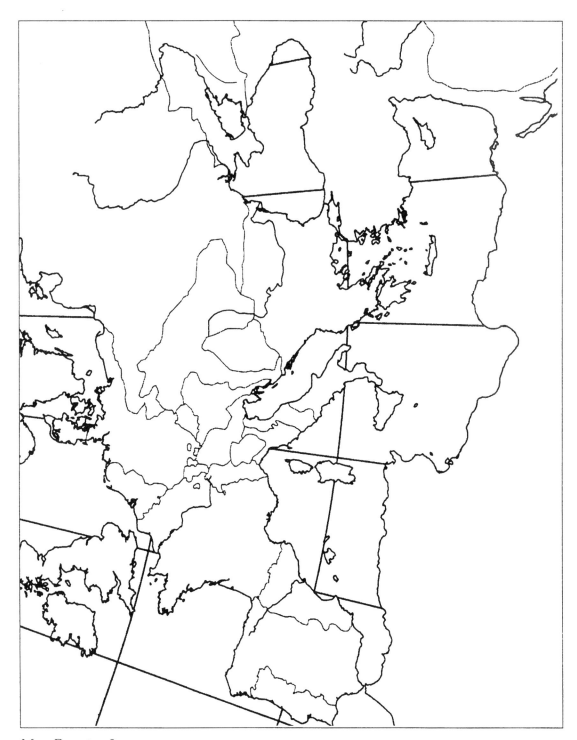

Map Exercise 8

Map Exercise 8:   The Empire of Charles V

Using various colors of pencil, shade and label the lands that by 1560 were Catholic, Anglican, Calvinist, and Lutheran. Then pinpoint and label the following cities:

1.   Amsterdam
2.   Dublin
3.   Edinburgh
4.   Geneva
5.   La Rochelle
6.   Madrid
7.   Oxford
8.   Rome
9.   Vienna
10.   Wittenberg
11.   Zurich

14 DISCOVERY AND CRISIS IN THE SIXTEENTH AND SEVENTEENTH CENTURIES

Chapter Outline:

I.   An Age of Discovery and Expansion
    A.   The Motives Behind Them
        1.   A Long-time Fascination with the East: Marco Polo
        2.   Hopes for Wealth through Trade
        3.   Christian Missions
        4.   The Technology Needed
    B.   The Portuguese Maritime Empire
        1.   Prince Henry, the Navigator
        2.   Bartolomeu Dias Around the Cape
        3.   Vasco da Gama to India
    C.   Voyages to the New World
        1.   Christopher Columbus
        2.   John Cabot
        3.   Ferdinand Magellan
        4.   The Treaty of Tordesillas
    D.   The Spanish Empire
        1.   Hernán Cortés and Mexico
        2.   Francisco Pizarro and Peru
    E.   Administration of the Empire
        1.   *Encomienda*
        2.   *Audiencias*
    F.   The Impact of Expansion
        1.   Destruction of Native Cultures
        2.   The Enrichment of Europe
        3.   National Rivalries

II.   Politics and Wars of Religion in the Sixteenth Century
    A.   The French Wars of Religion (1562-1598)
        1.   Catholics against Huguenots
        2.   Henry IV's Conversion to Catholicism
        3.   The Edict of Nantes
    B.   Spain's Philip II and Militant Catholicism
        1.   "The Most Catholic King" and Leader of the Holy League
        2.   Protestant Revolt in the Netherlands and William of Orange
    C.   Elizabeth's England
        1.   Act of Supremacy
        2.   The Spanish Armada

III.   Economic and Social Crises
    A.   Economic Declines
    B.   The Witchcraft Craze

IV.   Seventeenth-Century Crises: War and Rebellions
    A.   The Thirty Years' War (1618-1648)
    B.   Rebellions

V.   Culture in a Turbulent World
    A.   Art: Mannerism and Baroque
        1.   El Greco
        2.   Peter Paul Rubens
        3.   Gian Lorenzo Bernini
        4.   Artemesia Gentileschi
    B.   A Golden Age of Literature
        1.   England's William Shakespeare
        2.   Spain's Lope de Vega and Miguel de Cervantes

Chapter Summary:

The energies released by the Renaissance and the rivalries unleashed by the Reformation made the late sixteenth and seventeenth centuries a time of discovery, expansion, political chaos, and intellectual growth. It was an age of danger, opportunity, and achievement.

Portuguese and then Spanish explorers sailed around Africa to India and the Far East and then across the Atlantic to discover the Americas. Soon there were European empires in far places, and soon all of the nations of Europe were competing for trade routes and foreign colonies.

The Reformation, which had divided Europe into warring religious camps, now brought battles between and even within nation-states over which group taught the true Christian faith. The French and Spanish Catholic power structures sought to enforce their religious views on rebellious subjects—in France a Protestant minority called Huguenots, in Spanish territories a Dutch Protestant minority. In England, where the Elizabethan age had confirmed the nation's Protestantism, Catholics were subject to the same treatment Protestants received in France and Spain. The Holy Roman Empire, however, saw the most protracted and violent of the Religious Wars, one that lasted for thirty years. In the midst of all this chaos, both Protestants and Catholics turned their frustrations and hostilities on people they accused of practicing witchcraft.

Yet despite the turbulence of the day, the world of art, philosophy, and literature moved toward Enlightenment. El Greco, Rubens, and Bernini gave visible expression to the dreams of a harsh age, while Shakespeare and Cervantes fashioned literary masterpieces that shaped modern literature. It was a difficult age, but it was a wonderful age as well.

Identify:

1.   Henry the "Navigator"   [p. 282]

2.   Vasco da Gama   [p. 283-284]

3.   Columbus   [pp. 283-284]

4.   Treaty of Tordesillas   [p. 284]

5.   Huguenots   [pp. 288-289]

6.   Lepanto   [p. 289]

7.   William of Orange   [pp. 289-290]

8.   Spanish Armada   [p. 291]

9.   Peace of Westphalia   [p. 294]

10.   El Greco   [p. 297]

11.   Baroque   [pp. 298-299]

12.   Peter Paul Rubens   [p. 298]

13.   Lope de Vega   [p. 300]

14.   Cervantes   [p. 300]

Match the following words with their definitions:

1.	Ferdinand Magellan	A.	introduced the world to a man from La Mancha
2.	Treaty of Tordesillas	B.	painted a series of works on Old Testament heroines
3.	Francesco Pizarro	C.	this divided non-Christian lands between Spain and Portugal
4.	Edict of Nantes	D.	facilitated Shakespeare's theatrical career
5.	Peace of Westphalia	E.	Spanish explorer whose expedition was the first to circumnavigate the earth
6.	El Greco	F.	painter whose work captured the religious tensions and intense emotions of a turbulent age
7.	Gian Lorenzo Bernini	G.	this ended the Thirty Years' War
8.	Artemisia Gentileschi	H.	granted some freedom of religion to Huguenots
9.	Lord Chamberlain's Company	I.	Spanish general who conquered the Incan Empire
10.	Cervantes	J.	Baroque artist who completed the building of Saint Peter's Church

Multiple Choice:

1. Portugal's expansionism was motivated by

    a. zeal to convert Asians to the Catholic faith.
    b. a desire for profit in spices.
    c. the strong will of members of the royal family.
    d. all of the above

2.   Spanish expansion and exploration of the New World is best characterized by the

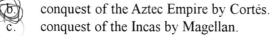

      a.   first circumnavigation of the globe by Amerigo Vespucci.
      b.   conquest of the Aztec Empire by Cortés.
      c.   conquest of the Incas by Magellan.
      d.   discovery of California by Pizarro.

3.   The name America that was given to the New World came from Amerigo Vespucci, who was

      a.   a Spanish pirate.
      b.   an Italian writer.
      c.   an Italian missionary.
      d.   a Portuguese governmental official.

4.   The French religious minority, the Huguenots, were spiritual descendants of

      a.   Thomas Aquinas.
      b.   Martin Luther.
      c.   Michel Montaigne.
      d.   John Calvin.

5.   The religious climate of France prior to the French Wars of Religion was best characterized by

      a.   a nobility that was nearly 50% Huguenot.
      b.   a population split evenly between Huguenots and Catholics.
      c.   complete suppression of Huguenots by the Bourbons.
      d.   a poorly organized Huguenot opposition to a Catholic majority.

6.   The French Wars of Religion from 1562 to 1598

      a.   ended with Henry of Navarre's Edict of Nantes.
      b.   saw the Huguenots win on the battlefield and force the Catholics to recognize them.
      c.   ended when the last of the Huguenots were killed.
      d.   were entirely French, without ties to conflicts elsewhere.

7.   The witch hunts of the sixteenth and seventeenth centuries

      a.   grew out of social unrest due to the shift from a communal to an individualist society.
      b.   were directed at the wealthy by their jealous neighbors.
      c.   were in no way sanctioned by organized religious groups.
      d.   were restricted to rural areas.

8. Witchcraft hysteria declined in part because

    a. women organized for self-defense.
    b. destruction brought by the religious wars made people more tolerant.
    c. a papal decree condemned violence against social misfits.
    d. covens were all destroyed.

9. As a result of the Thirty Years' War and the Peace of Westphalia in 1648

    a. the German economy was totally destroyed.
    b. each German state could choose its own religion.
    c. the growing gulf between religious and political motives became clear.
    d. the Holy Roman Empire was made secure for another hundred years.

10. The late sixteenth and early seventeenth centuries were a time of

    a. great accomplishments in English theater.
    b. decline in theater everywhere due to Puritanism.
    c. new directions in Latin literature.
    d. a return to the morality plays of the Middle Ages.

Complete the following sentences:

1. Encouraged by the support of Prince Henry, known as the ___Navigator___, Portuguese sailor ___Vasco___ ___de___ ___Gama___ found a sea route to India, where Alfonso _____ _____ set up the beginnings of an empire.

2. In the Americas, Spaniard ___Hernán___ ___Cortes___ conquered the Aztecs, while _____ _____ conquered the Incas. In both places the Spanish crown instituted a social and economic system called the _____.

3. The Edict of Nantes permitted the French ___Huguenots___ to ___practice___ freely and to hold _____ _____.

4. In 1559 the English parliament passed a new Act of _____, making Queen ___Elizabeth___ both spiritual and temporal ruler, ending the Catholic policies of her sister ___Mary___.

5. In 1588 Philip II sent an ___Armada___ to invade England and restore the ___Catholic___ Church, but it was battered by storms off the coasts of _____ and _____.

6.   The Thirty Years War, considered the last of the _____ wars, began with a dispute in _____ lands and ended with the Peace of _____.

7.   Doménikos Theotocópoulos, known to the world of art as _____ _____, brought the _____ style to its level while working in the Spanish city _____.

8.   In his great Roman basilica, Bernini created a _____ for Saint Peter, which hovered in air, supported by four great _____ of the church.

9.   Shakespeare came to London in the reign of _____ and wrote plays for his _____ _____ Company, which performed in such theaters as the _____ and _____.

10.   In his masterpiece, Miguel de Cervantes had his character _____ _____ represent lofty ideals, while the squire _____ _____ represented hard-headed realism.

Place the following in chronological order and give dates:

1.   Edict of Nantes   1.

2.   United Provinces of the Netherlands proclaimed   2.

3.   Shakespeare's arrival in London   3.

4.   Treaty of Tordesillas   4.

5.   Defeat of the Spanish Armada   5.

6.   Peace of Westphalia   6.

7.   Diaz rounds Cape of Good Hope   7.

Questions for Critical Thought: In each essay fully explore the topic by answering the questions that follow it.

1.   The Spanish Empire. What motivated the Spanish to set out on voyages of discovery and conquest? Who were the major agents of this enterprise, and what did they add to Spain's territory? What kind of governmental, economic, and social system did the Spanish create for their empire? How did this period affect the development of the Americas?

2.   French and English Religious Settlements. How did the French under Henry IV resolve their religious wars? How did the English under Elizabeth resolve theirs? How were the resolutions alike, and how were they different? How final were they?

3.   The Great Witch Hunt. What caused the witchcraft scare of the seventeenth century? What conditions fueled it, and why did it finally end? Who suffered and why? What does it say about European society at the time?

4.   The Golden Age of European Literature. What did Shakespeare and Cervantes add to the literary tradition of Western Europe? How did their careers and achievements differ? How do their differences reflect the characters of their two countries?

Analysis of Primary Source Documents:

1.   What did Cortés think of the Aztec civilization he conquered? What made him feel justified in destroying it? What does this say about his own Spanish civilization?

2.   From the witchcraft case you have read, what "rules" of law did the witch hunters of the seventeenth century follow? How would a modern defense attorney attack their case?

3.   Describe the treatment of peasants on the farm captured by foreign soldiers during the Thirty Years' War, as recounted in the book *Simplicius Simplicissimus*. To what extent do you see exaggeration for effect, and to what extent does this account agree with what you have read of treatment of civilians in other wars?

4.   How much of Shakespeare's tribute to England in *Richard II* is patriotism, how much xenophobia, and how much the dramatist's wish to please his audience? Give reasons for your opinion.

Map Exercise 9

Map Exercise 9: European Overseas Possessions in 1658

Using various colors of pencil, shade and label the following:

1. Angola
2. Brazil
3. Canton
4. India
5. Indonesia
6. New Spain
7. Philippines

Pinpoint and label the following:

1. Calicut
2. Cape of Good Hope
3. Colombo
4. Hispaniola
5. Macao
5. Tenochtitlán

CHAPTER 15

RESPONSE TO CRISIS: STATE BUILDING AND THE SEARCH FOR ORDER IN THE SEVENTEENTH CENTURY

Chapter Outline:

I.   The Practice of Absolutism: Western Europe
   A.   France and Absolute Monarchy
      1.   Cardinal Richelieu's Centralization of Power under Louis XIII
      2.   Cardinal Mazarin during the Minority of Louis XIV
      3.   The Reign of Louis XIV (1643-1715)
         a.   Control of the Nobility: Versailles
         b.   Colbert and Mercantilism
   B.   The Decline of Spain
      1.   Reforms by Guzmán
      2.   Wars and Revolts

II. Absolutism in Central, Eastern, and Northern Europe
   A.   The German States
      1.   Brandenburg-Prussia
         a.   The House of Hohenzollern
         b.   Frederick William's Army and His Commissariat
         c.   Elector Frederick III Becomes King Frederick I
      2.   The Emergence of Austria
         a.   The House of Habsburg
         b.   Leopold I's Move to the East
         c.   A Multiculture Empire
   B.   From Muscovy to Russia
      1.   The Reign of Ivan the Terrible
      2.   Michael and the Romanovs

Chapter Summary:

The political and religious crises of the sixteenth and early seventeenth centuries led philosophers and rulers to consider alternatives to what they considered the insecure and often chaotic institutional structures of the day. For over a century both groups defended the growth of power at the top, strong monarchies that could keep the peace and order, who could enforce social uniformity, who could take measures to increase national prosperity.

Government moved increasingly toward absolutism, toward kings stronger than any known in Europe before, toward kings with power to provide order and prosperity. While absolutism reached its apex in France with the reign of Louis XIV, it had significant successes in Spain, the German states, Italy, Russia, and the Ottoman Empire. Everywhere there was a movement toward centralized power, the weakening of local rulers, and state control of economies.

Only in a few nations did royal power diminish and begin to share rule with parliamentary and constitutional systems: in the United Provinces of Holland, and most importantly in Britain. From the days of the first Stuart, James I, king and Parliament shared a "balanced polity." James' son Charles

I tried to usurp Parliament's power and was beheaded. After eleven years Parliament "restored" the Stuarts to power; but there occurred in 1688 a bloodless revolt against the Catholic James II, whom Parliament replaced with the dual monarchy of William and Mary, who promised certain rights to Parliament and British citizens. There the way was paved not only for limited monarchy but also for democracy.

This Age of Absolutism was an age of cultural and philosophical achievement. It was the Golden Age of Dutch painting, exemplified by the work of Rembrandt. It was an age when the French theater gained world dominance, as demonstrated by the work of Molière. It was a time of ferment in political theory, exemplified by the absolutist conjectures of Thomas Hobbes and the social contract of John Locke. In many ways the Enlightenment was beginning.

Identify:

1.   Absolutism [p. 304]

2.   Richelieu [p. 304]

3.   Colbert [p. 307]

4.   Gaspar de Guzmán [p. 309]

5.   Hohenzollerns [pp. 309-310]

6.   Habsburgs [p. 310]

7.   Ivan the Terrible [p. 311]

8.   Streltsy [p. 313]

9.   "Glorious" Revolution [p. 318]

10.   Toleration Act [pp. 318-319]

11.   *Leviathan* [p. 319]

12.   Mercantilism [p. 320]

13.   Rembrandt [p. 322]

14.   Molière [p. 323]

Match the following words with their definitions:

1. Mazarin

2. Fronde

3. Versailles

4. Cromwell

5. Bill of Rights

6. Thomas Hobbes

7. John Locke

8. Mercantilism

9. Judith Leyster

10. Molière

A. argued that if a monarch broke his social contract, the people had the right to form a new government

B. granted Parliament the power to levy taxes

C. leader of the British Commonwealth

D. belief that a nation's wealth depends on its gold and silver reserves

E. he argued that order demanded absolute monarchy

F. playwright who satirized religion and society

G. center of Louis XIV's royal government

H. a rebellion of the French nobility against the royal family

I. member of the Guild of St. Luke in Haarlem who captured everyday Dutch life in paintings

J. he dominated the French government when Louis XIV was a child

Multiple Choice:

1. One result of the seventeenth century crises in Europe was

    a. an increased role of churches in secular society.
    b. a trend toward democratic reforms in government.
    c. the division of empires into smaller feudal kingdoms.
    d. a trend toward absolutism, as exemplified by Louis XIV.

2. As Louis XIII's chief minister, Cardinal Richelieu was most successful in

    a. evicting the Huguenots from France.
    b. strengthening the central role of the monarchy.
    c. creating a reservoir of funds for the treasury.
    d. emerging victorious in the Fronde revolts.

3.   Louis XIV restructured the policy-making machinery of the French government by

    a.   personally dominating the actions of his ministers and secretaries.
    b.   stacking the royal council with high nobles and royal princes.
    c.   selecting his ministers from established aristocratic families.
    d.   all of the above

4.   Louis XIV's military adventures resulted in

    a.   French domination of Western Europe.
    b.   defeat after defeat by coalitions of nations.
    c.   the union of the thrones of France and Spain.
    d.   increased popular support of Louis in France.

5.   The overall practical purpose of the Versailles system was to

    a.   exclude the high nobility from real power.
    b.   serve as a hospital for Louis when he was ill.
    c.   act as a reception hall for foreign visitors.
    d.   give Louis a life of absolute privacy.

6.   The social reforms of Peter the Great

    a.   failed to change habits of dress and grooming.
    b.   left the Orthodox Church untouched.
    c.   required Russian men to wear beards.
    d.   permitted Russian women many new freedoms.

7.   Peter the Great's primary foreign policy goal was

    a.   to open a warm-water port accessible to Europe for Russia.
    b.   the utter destruction of the Ottoman Empire.
    c.   victory and control over the Scandinavian countries.
    d.   the conquest of Germany.

8.   The British Bill of Rights

    a.   laid the foundation for a constitutional monarchy.
    b.   resolved England's seventeenth-century religious feuds.
    c.   reaffirmed the divine-right theory of kingship.
    d.   gave the king the right to raise armies without consent of Parliament.

9. Thomas Hobbes' *Leviathan* was a

    a. sea snake that killed a little Dutch boy.
    b. mythical Frankish king, a role model for James II.
    c. state with the power to keep order.
    d. principle of the right to revolution.

10. The mercantilist policies that dominated Europe's economy in the seventeenth century

    a. concerned itself with the changing volume of trade.
    b. stressed co-prosperity among nations through fair trading practices.
    c. were responsible for great economic and population growth through the century.
    d. stressed the role of the state in the successful conduct of economic affairs.

Complete the following sentences:

1. Henry IV had granted French Huguenots civil rights with his Edict of _____, but Louis XIV took them away with his Edict of _____.

2. Jean-Baptiste Colbert, controller-general of _____ for Louis XIV, followed the policy of _____, encouraging _____, discouraging _____.

3. Spanish Count Guzmán tried to energize his country with a series of _____ _____ but was thwarted by conservative Spanish _____.

4. The Hohenzollern ruler who built Prussia was the Great Elector _____ _____, who based his strength on a large and efficient _____ and used a _____ to raise revenues.

5. Peter Romanov decided after a trip to _____ Europe that Russia was socially and economically _____ and needed reform. He adopted a _____ economic policy and established a _____ _____ to make decisions for the Church.

6. During its Commonwealth period, England was ruled by the soldier _____ _____, who dismissed _____ and ruled with the aid of a group of military _____.

7. When it became evident to the English that James II's baby son would perpetuate a _____ dynasty, a revolution exiled him in favor of William of _____ and his wife _____, who was the daughter of James II.

8. American and French revolutionaries used Englishman John Locke's theories to demand _____ government, the rule of _____, and protection of _____.

9. The Golden Age of Dutch painting was paralleled by the supremacy of Dutch _____ and reached its height with the work of _____.

10. Molière got away with satirizing court life in his play *The* _____, but he was in hot water when his *Tartuffe* made fun of the _____.

Place the following in chronological order and give dates:

1. Peter Romanov's trip to the West   1.

2. Execution of Charles I   2.

3. Turkish siege of Vienna   3.

4. England's Glorious Revolution   4.

5. Publication of Hobbes' *Leviathan*   5.

6. Frederick III becomes Frederick I   6.

7. Edict of Fontainebleau   7.

Questions for Critical Thought: In each essay fully explore the topic by answering the questions that follow it.

1. Absolutism: Theory and Practice. What conditions led to the establishment of absolutist monarchies? How did the Englishman Thomas Hobbes justify them? How did two absolutists, Louis XIV and Peter I, achieve the degrees of absolute control they enjoyed? How did each control the various elements of society that might have opposed them? What legacies did they leave their nations?

2. The Transformation of Brandenburg-Prussia. Brandenburg-Prussia was transformed from what to what in the seventeenth and eighteenth centuries? How did this happen? What made the transformation possible? Who was responsible? What did it mean for Europe's future?

3. Peter Romanov and the Rise of Russia. What were Peter's dreams for his country? How did he go about realizing them? What policies did he pursue to reach them? What kind of nation did he leave when he died?

4.   The Limits of Absolutism. Why did nations such as Britain and the Netherlands not follow the path to absolute monarchy? What institutions and traditions prevented it? How were they able to retain order without monarchist authority? How did the work and theories of John Locke both reflect British reality and affect future thinking about authority?

Analysis of Primary Source Documents:

1.   How do Louis XIV's *Memoirs* show that he had given some thought to the duties of a king? How well did his theory fit his actions?

2.   Explain how Peter Romanov's treatment of the rebellious Streltsy might prove Machiavelli's contention that the effective ruler must act without consideration for the usual principles of morality or ethics.

3.   Explain how the 1688 British Bill of Rights paved the way for constitutional government. Show how this Bill influenced the thoughts of American colonists in the next century.

4.   What do the letters from the two kings tell you about the personalities of those kings and about the characters of their respective countries?

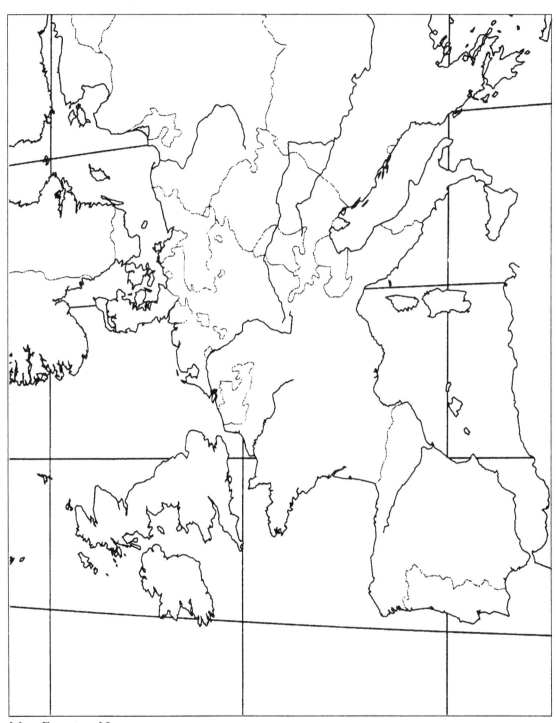

Map Exercise 10

Map Exercise 10: Europe in 1648

Using various colors of pencil, shade and label the following:

1.   Bohemia
2.   Brandenburg
3.   Poland
4.   Prussia
5.   Russian Empire
6.   Spanish Netherlands
7.   Swiss Cantons
8.   Transylvania
9.   United Provinces

Pinpoint and label the following:

1.   Amsterdam
2.   Berlin
3.   Brussels
4.   Prague
5.   Warsaw

CHAPTER

16 TOWARD A NEW HEAVEN AND A NEW EARTH: THE SCIENTIFIC REVOLUTION AND THE EMERGENCE OF MODERN SCIENCE

Chapter Outline:

IV. Women in the Origins of Modern Science
    A. Informal Educations and Exclusion from Universities
    B. Margaret Cavendish
    C. Maria Winkelmann and the Berlin Academy

V. Toward a New Earth: Descartes, Rationalism, and a New View of Humankind
    A. Descartes' *Discourse on Method*
    B. The Implications of Cartesian Dualism

VI. Science and Religion in the Seventeenth Century
    A. The Example of Galileo
    B. Blaise Pascal and his *Pensées*

VII. The Spread of Scientific Knowledge
    A. Scientific Method: Bacon and Descartes
    B. Scientific Societies
    C. Science and Society

Chapter Summary:

At the same time that kings were consolidating power and seeking a new social order based on absolute rule, an intellectual revolution was taking place that would change educated people's understanding of the universe, of man's nature, and even of the nature of truth itself. This revolution in science provided new models both for heaven and for earth.

The Scientific Revolution began with astronomy, and conclusions drawn by mathematicians and observers like Copernicus, Kepler, Galileo, and Newton both provided new understandings of the universe and its laws and called into question the wisdom of ancient and medieval scholars. From the study of astronomy and the realization that by empirical observation one can know the truth about the universe, various scholars, male and female, began questioning and revising opinions about medicine and the human sciences.

Parallel to the revolution in imperial studies was a new emphasis on human reason. Started by Rene Descartes and his famous *Discourse on Method*, the new claims for rationalism focused attention on the nature and capacities of mankind. While empiricism and rationalism were at times in conflict, they eventually merged to create a scholarship that rejected both tradition and authority in favor of continual reevaluation of established knowledge.

Religious sensitivities were ruffled by these secular endeavors, and scientists often found themselves at odds with religious powers. Even some of the scientists themselves were disturbed by the results of their studies. Pascal dedicated his life to the reconciliation of science and religion, but his life was too brief to develop all of his ideas fully.

Yet science was too careful about its conclusions to be discredited and proved itself too useful to the world to be silenced. Scientific societies, sponsored by kings, disseminated discoveries, and the general public benefited from what the scientists were doing. The modern world of progress and doubt was on its way.

Identify:

1.   Hermetic   [p. 327]

2.   Geocentric   [pp. 327-328]

3.   Heliocentric   [pp. 327-329]

4.   Music of the Spheres   [p. 328]

5.   *Principia*   [pp. 331-332]

6.   Galen   [p. 332]

7.   Andreas Vesalius   [pp. 332-333]

8.   Harvey   [pp. 332-333]

9.   Margaret Cavendish   [pp. 333-334]

10.   Maria Winkelmann   [p. 334]

11.   Descartes   [p. 336]

12.   Pascal   [pp. 337-338]

13.   Bacon   [p. 339]

14.   Royal Society   [p. 339]

Match the following words with their definitions:

1. Nicholas Copernicus

2. Johannes Kepler

3. *The Starry Messenger*

4. Isaac Newton

5. Vesalius

6. William Harvey

7. Margaret Cavendish

8. Maria Winkelmann

9. Rene Descartes

10. *Pensées*

A. advocated a geometric universe and tried to discover the "music of the spheres"

B. discovered the circulation of blood and showed it was caused by the pumping of the heart

C. an astronomer denied a post in the Berlin Academy

D. began a systematic dissection of human bodies

E. an attempt to reconcile science and religion

F. scientist excluded from the Royal Society

G. Cambridge scholar who first explained universal gravitation

H. through mathematical calculations came to regard Ptolomy's geocentric universe as too complicated

I. an advocate of rationalism who began his method with doubt of all things

J. a defense of the Copernican system

Multiple Choice:

1. The Scientific Revolution of the seventeenth century was

    a. stimulated by new confirmations of the work of Ptolemy and Galen.
    b. a direct result of the revolt against social conditions in the Middle Ages.
    c. born in the new intellectual monasteries.
    d. more a gradual building on the accomplishments of previous centuries than a sudden shift in thought.

2.   The greatest achievements in science during the sixteenth and seventeenth centuries came in which three areas?

    a.   astronomy, mechanics, medicine
    b.   astronomy, biology, chemistry
    c.   biology, mechanics, ballistics
    d.   engineering, physics, dentistry

3.   The general conception of the universe before Copernicus held that

    a.   the sun was at the center and the earth circled it.
    b.   the earth was at a stationary center, while perfect crystalline spheres orbited it.
    c.   the earth rested on the shell of a giant turtle.
    d.   it was all a mystery known only to theologians.

4.   The universal theories proposed by Copernicus

    a.   led to his arrest and imprisonment in a monastery.
    b.   were supported by Protestants in order to make the Catholics look foolish.
    c.   made the universe less complicated by rejecting Ptolemy's epicycles.
    d.   explained the appearance of the sun's rotation with a theory of earthly rotation.

5.   Galileo held that the planets were

    a.   composed of material much like that of earth.
    b.   reflections of the divine city.
    c.   spheres composed of pure energy.
    d.   merely mirages in the "desert" of space.

6.   Isaac Newton's scientific discoveries

    a.   were met with more hostility in England than on the continent of Europe.
    b.   formed the basis for universal physics until well into the twentieth century.
    c.   completely divorced God from the universe and its laws.
    d.   were the first to be printed in a language other than Latin.

7.   Newton's universal law of gravity

    a.   offered an explanation for all motion in the universe.
    b.   had little practical application to the questions of universal motion.
    c.   showed that humans could never understand why God made things the way they are.
    d.   seemed to indicate that the universe began with a "big bang."

8. Francis Bacon was important to the Scientific Revolution because of his emphasis on

   a. empirical, experimental observation.
   b. pure, theoretical reasoning.
   c. deductive conclusions, which moved from general to particular principles.
   d. the need for scientists to preserve nature.

9. Blaise Pascal believed that human beings

   a. can know God through pure reason.
   b. are as irrational as animals.
   c. can understand only what is revealed to them in the Bible.
   d. can go beyond reason to truth through faith.

10. Science became an integral part of Western culture in the eighteenth century because

   a. people came to see it as the only way to find the truth.
   b. its mechanistic theories were popular with kings.
   c. it offered a new means of exploiting nature for profit.
   d. radical groups like the Levellers, when they came to power, insisted on the supremacy of science.

Complete the following sentences:

1. Renaissance humanists demonstrated that not all ancient scholars agreed with the scientific conclusions of _____ and _____, who had been unquestioned in medieval science. Renaissance artists stimulated science through their close observation of _____ and human _____.

2. Leonardo da Vinci reasoned that since God eternally _____, nature is inherently _____. At the same time many scientists still sought the secrets of the universe through _____ magic.

3. Copernicus rejected Ptolemy's _____ universe and postulated a _____ one because he found Ptolemy's system too _____.

4. Peering through his telescope, Galileo discovered _____ on the moon, Jupiter's four _____, and _____ spots.

5. Newton believed the universe to be a divinely regulated _____ and was characterized by _____ time and space. His universal law of _____ seemed to prove him correct.

6.   Vesalius disputed Galen's assertion that blood vessels originate in the _____ but did not doubt his claim that two different kinds of blood flow through the _____ and _____.

7.   Maria Winkelmann proved her skill in the field of _____, yet she was rejected when she applied for a post at the _____ _____ because she was a _____.

8.   Descartes argued that the _____ of man cannot be doubted but that the _____ _____ can and should be, thus creating what we call Cartesian _____.

9.   Pascal was trying to bridge the gap between the new _____ and the traditional _____ faith in his unfinished work _____.

10.   Francis Bacon said science must be based on organized _____, using sensual _____ and _____ reasoning.

Place the following in chronological order and give dates:

1.   Harvey's *On the Motion of the*   1.
      Heart and Blood published

2.   Newton's *Principia* completed   2.

3.   Copernicus' *On the Revolutions of the* 3.
      Heavenly Spheres published

4.   Bacon leaves *The Great Instauration* unfinished   4.

5.   Descartes' *Discourse on Method* written   5.

6.   Pascal's *Pensées* left unfinished   6.

7.   Galileo's *The Starry Messenger* published   7.

Questions for Critical Thought: In each essay fully explore the topic by answering the questions that follow it.

1.   The Scientific Revolution. What led to the scientific revolution of the seventeenth century? Which early scientific assumptions sound logical and which sound illogical to a modern mind?

Who were the pioneers of this revolution, and what did they discover? Why did astronomy lead the way and medicine follow? How did this period affect the modern world?

2.   Women in Early Science. What credentials did Cavendish and Winkelmann bring to the scientific profession? What did they achieve? Why were they not recognized by the scientific establishment of their day? How did they react?

3.   Doubters in the Scientific Revolution. What doubts did Descartes and Pascal, from their differing perspectives, express about the bright future of science? How valid did each man's criticism prove to be? What made science go forward and succeed despite its critics? Does either man's ideas have relevance today?

Analysis of Primary Source Documents:

1.   Explain Copernicus' heliocentric theory of the universe and show why scientists of his day found it to be at the same time so simple and so profound.

2.   What personality traits can you find in Galileo's account of his astronomical observations that would explain why he was a successful scientist?

3.   Speculate on why—amid the scientific progress of his times—Spinoza was so unprepared to accept women as equals.

4.   What was at the root of Pascal's doubts about man's ability to find scientific certainty? What problems for science of the future did he accurately pose?

17 THE EIGHTEENTH CENTURY: AN AGE OF ENLIGHTENMENT

Chapter Outline:

I. The Enlightenment
    A. "Dare to Know"
    B. The Paths to the Enlightenment
        1. Popular Understanding and Acceptance of Science: Fontenelle
        2. A New Skepticism about Religion and Tradition
        3. Broader Travel and Literature that Disseminated Knowledge
        4. Isaac Newton's Laws of Physics
        5. John Locke's Theory of Knowledge
    C. The Philosophes and Their Ideas
        1. Montesquieu's Critique of Society and Government
        2. Voltaire's Critique of Justice and Religion
        3. Diderot's *Encyclopedia* and a New Way of Thinking
    D. Toward a New "Science of Man"
        1. Quesnay and Laws Governing the Economy
        2. Adam Smith and a Study of *The Wealth of Nations*
    E. The Later Enlightenment and Rousseau
    F. The "Women's Question" in the Enlightenment
        1. Mary Astell and Sexual Equality
        2. Mary Wollstonecraft and Feminism
    G. The Social Environment of the Philosophes
        1. The Salon
        2. Coffee Houses and Secret Societies

II. Culture and Society in an Age of Enlightenment
    A. Innovations in Art, Music, and Literature
        1. The Rococo Art of Watteau, Tiepolo, and Neumann
        2. The Music of Bach, Handel, Haydn, and Mozart
        3. The Novel

B.   The High Culture of the Eighteenth Century
C.   Popular Culture: Festivals and Taverns
D.   Crime and Punishment: Cesare Beccaria

III.   Religion and the Churches
A.   Toleration and Religious Minorities
B.   Popular Religion
1.   Catholic Piety and Saints
2.   Protestant Revivalism and John Wesley

Chapter Summary:

Each age builds upon the foundations of its predecessor, and never was this true to a greater degree than the way the eighteenth century built upon the seventeenth. The seventeenth century's revolution in science led directly to the eighteenth century's Enlightenment revolution in philosophy.

The popularization of science, the growth of a healthy skepticism about tradition, the writings of world travelers, and the legacy of thinkers like John Locke and Isaac Newton brought about an eighteenth century flowering of philosophy, which is considered one of the high points of Western civilization. The philosophes—Montesquieu, Voltaire, Diderot, Adam Smith, and Rousseau—left a body of thought and writing that is unsurpassed in the history of social criticism.

It was also an age of innovation in the arts. Rococo painting and architecture, classical music, and the birth of the novel form in literature all added style and color to the age. In the social sciences, various writers began critically commenting on education, crime and punishment, and the social and economic causes behind historical events. The stage was set for modern scholarship and social criticism.

Christianity, which the philosophes blamed for many human woes, found itself in a hostile environment, with the institutional church branded archaic and intellectuals leaving it for what they considered a more respectable deism. Yet among the common people the traditional faith continued to have strong appeal and tenacity. A new era of piety swept both Protestant and Catholic camps; England particularly experienced a new phenomenon—the popular revival meetings of John Wesley.

The Enlightenment of the eighteenth century was the product of a revolution in science, and the ideas it so freely disseminated helped usher in the age of political revolution to come. It was both the child and the parent of revolution.

Identify:

1.   Enlightenment [pp. 344-346]

2.   Montesquieu [p. 347]

3.   Denis Diderot [p. 349] *Encyclopedia – ideas of the Enlightenment were spread even further.*
Freelance writer – Christianity (fanatical & unreasonable)
– deism–atheism "The world is only a mass of molecules"

4.   Social Contract [pp. 350-351]
(Jean-Jacques Rousseau (pub. 1762) tried to harmonize individual liberty with governmental authority
– an agreement on the part of an entire society to be governed by its general will

Madame Geoffrin

5.   Salon [pp. 352-353]
elegant drawing rooms in the homes of the wealthy, where the philosophes were invited gathered to discuss
the new ideas of the philosophes. provided havens for people + ideas unwelcome in the royal court.

6.   Rococo [pp. 353-354] *– run by women*
– a new style, emphasizing grace & gentle action, curves, followed the wandering lines of
natural objects such as seashells & flowers "pleasure, happiness + love"

7.   Balthasar Neumann [p. 354]
– German architect
– Vierzehnheiligen (church in Germany Baroque-Rococo)

8.   *The Messiah* [p. 355]
– George Frederick Handel (Germany)

9.   Mozart [p. 355] *Wolfgang Amadeus Mozart The marriage of Figaro Don Giovanni The magic flute*
– classical composer, rather than Baroque – melody, blend of grace
– music centre of Europe shifted from Italy to the Austrian Empire

10.   Carnival [p. 356]
– celebrated in the Mediterranean world of Spain, Italy, France, Germany, Austria
– began on the first day of the year, lasted until the first day of Lent

11.   Cesare Beccaria [p. 357] *– a time of great indulgence, before abstaining during Lent*
– Italian philosophe   – against capital punishment
"On Crimes + Punishment" – punishment should only serve as deterrents, not as exercises in brutality

12.   Methodism [pp. 358-359]
– rival of Christianity – John Wesley (England)
– "saved from experiencing God + opening the doors to his grace"
– conversion experience = violent + emotional

Match the following words with their definitions:

1. *Persian Letters*

2. Deism

3. *Emile*

4. Mary Astell

5. Balthasar Neumann

6. J. S. Bach

7. G. F. W. Handel

8. W. A. Mozart

9. Carnival

10. Beccaria

A. composer of the Baroque *St. Matthew's Passion*

B. composer

C. a social antidote to Lent

D. belief in god the Creator without reference to Christian dogma

E. critique of French society and religion

F. reformer who criticized practices of punishment for crimes

G. Rococo architect who built the Würzburg Residenz

H. advocated better education for women

I. Rousseau's imaginary student in his book on education

J. prodigy who composed *The Marriage of Figaro*

Multiple-Choice:

1. The Enlightenment of the eighteenth century was characterized by the philosophes'

    a. naïve optimism that they could change society.
    b. rejection of traditional Christian dogma.
    c. emphasis on mysticism rather than rationalism.
    d. revival of medieval Scholasticism.

2. The French philosophes

    a. fashioned a grand, rational system of thought.
    b. flourished in an atmosphere of government support.
    c. called for the state to suppress ideas contrary to their own.
    d. left families behind to live in communes.

3.   In his *Spirit of the Laws*, Montesquieu was above all concerned with

    a.   supporting a strong monarchy.
    b.   supporting a dominant legislature.
    c.   elevating the judiciary to absolute power.
    d.   maintaining a balance between the three branches of government.

4.   Voltaire was perhaps best known for his criticism of

    a.   the German state and its militarism.
    b.   the modern idea of separation of church and state.
    c.   religious and social intolerance.
    d.   Renaissance intellectual excesses.

5.   In his *Social Contract*, Rousseau expressed the belief that

    a.   government is an evil that should be eliminated.
    b.   the will of the individual is all-important.
    c.   we achieve freedom by following what is best for all.
    d.   a child is a small adult with all the same abilities and obligations.

6.   Rococo architecture of the eighteenth century was

    a.   largely confined to France.
    b.   best expressed in the work of Baron d'Holbach.
    c.   best expressed in the work of Balthasar Neumann.
    d.   characterized by strict geometrical patterns.

7.   European music of the eighteenth century was exemplified by

    a.   Amadeus Mozart, who shifted the musical focus from Italy to Austria.
    b.   G.F.W. Handel, a prince who composed as a hobby.
    c.   the elitist, aristocratic world of Haydn.
    d.   the loosely woven, secular odes of Bach.

8.   Cesare Beccaria argued that treatment of criminals should

    a.   include capital punishment.
    b.   impress the mind without tormenting the body.
    c.   be swift and brutal.
    d.   vary according to the criminal's class.

9. Most eighteenth-century Christians believed that the solution to the "Jewish problem" was

    a. complete religious tolerance in each nation.
    b. conversion to the Christian faith.
    c. exile to the Americas or Africa.
    e. camps for mass extermination.

10. His own Anglican Church regarded John Wesley's movement as a

    a. dangerous heretical sect.
    b. political uprising.
    c. lot of emotional, superstitious nonsense.
    d. valuable tool for giving the Church more energy.

Complete the following sentences:

1. Fontenelle used a conversation between an aristocratic _lady_ and her _astronomer friend_ to teach about the _new_ _cosmology_.

2. In his *Persian Letters*, Montesquieu criticized the two main French institutions, the _catholic_ _church_ and the French _monarchy_. In his *Spirit of the Laws* he praised British government for its _greater freedom_ and _security of a state_.

3. Voltaire, whose religious faith is termed _deism_, saw God as a Divine _machine/mechanic_. He called on his readers to _____ organized religion.

4. Diderot's great multi-volume contribution to the Enlightenment, his _encyclopedia_, attacked religious _superstitions_ and preached _toleration_.

5. Among the Physiocrats, Scotsman Adam Smith and Frenchman François Quesnay repudiated _mercantilism_ and said the state should be a _____ _____ that leaves the economy alone.

6. Jean-Jacques Rousseau's interests roamed from government in his book *The _Social_ _Contract_* to education in his _Emile_; and he blamed _____ _____ for the inequality of human society.

7. Rococo's grace is illustrated by Watteau's lyrical portrayals of _aristocratic_ life and Newmann's pilgrimage Church of the _Vierzehnheiligen_.

8.   Music lovers today still enjoy the genius of Bach's _St. Matthew's_ Passion, Handel's oratorio, The _Messiah_, and Mozart's opera _Don Giovanni_.

9.   Common people of the eighteenth century celebrated festivals such as _Carnival_, a time of excessive _____ activity and _indulgence_ of food and drink.

10.   Cesare Beccaria believed punishments should serve as _deterrents_, not as exercises in _brutality_, and he especially opposed _capital punishment_.

Place the following in chronological order and give dates:

1.   Publication of Adam Smith's _Wealth of Nations_ 177_   1.

2.   Publication of Rousseau's _Social Contract_ 176_   2.

3.   Publication of Montesquieu's _Persian Letters_   3.

4.   John Locke writes _Essay Concerning Human Understanding_   4.

5.   Publication of Wollstonecraft's _Vindication of_ 179_ _the Rights of Women_   5.

6.   Diderot's _Encyclopedia_ was begun 175_   6.

7.   Publication of Voltaire's _Treatise on Toleration_   7.

Questions for Critical Thought: In each essay, fully explore the topic by answering the questions that follow it.

1.   The Enlightenment. What social and intellectual changes in Europe led to the philosophical flowering called the Enlightenment? Who were the major figures of this era, and what did each add to the intellectual mix? How did their writings help fashion the modern world?

2.   The "New Science of Man." What were the roots of the new way of viewing human society? Who were the major figures in the new science, and what did each add to it? How did it lead to a new study of women? What are its influences on modern life?

3. The Golden Age of Music. What styles of music were prominent in this period? Who were the major composers, and what did they compose? Why are their names still known and their works still performed and appreciated today?

4. Popular Culture in a Time of Enlightenment. How did the culture of peasants differ from that of the intelligentsia during the Enlightenment? How did Carnival reflect what the lower classes enjoyed and how they found fulfillment? What forms did religious practice take in these classes? How did the Methodist movement fit into this pattern?

Analysis of Primary Source Documents:

1. What literary devices did Voltaire use to attack Christian intolerance? How would an orthodox Christian have answered him?

2. Briefly state the two arguments: that Rousseau's "general will" a) leads to democracy; b) leads to totalitarianism. Which argument is strongest?

3. Show how Mary Wollstonecraft appealed to both men and women in her call for the rights of women. What kinds of people (men and women) would have responded favorably, and what kinds would have responded unfavorably to her arguments?

4. Describe the church services conducted by John Wesley and his Methodists. Why did Wesley's Church of England not welcome this movement?

18 THE EIGHTEENTH CENTURY: EUROPEAN STATES, INTERNATIONAL WARS, AND SOCIAL CHANGE

Chapter Outline:

I. The European States
   A. Enlightened Absolutism?
   B. The Atlantic Seaboard States
      1. France and the Long Rule of Louis XV
      2. Great Britain and the Relations of King and Parliament
   C. Absolutism in Central and Eastern Europe
      1. Prussia: The Army and the Bureaucracy
      2. Austrian Empire of the Habsburgs
      3. Russia under Catherine the Great
   D. Enlightened Absolutism Revisited
      1. Rarity and Brevity
      2. Barriers of Reality

II. Wars and Diplomacy
   A. The War of the Austrian Succession (1740-1748)
   B. The Seven Years' War (1756-1763)
      1. The Theaters of War
      2. The War for Empire
      3. The British Victory

III. Economic Expansion and Social Change
   A. Population and Food
      1. A Falling Death Rate
      2. Improvements in Diet
   B. New Methods of Finance and Industry
      1. Public and Private Banks
      2. Textiles and Cottage Industries

C.   A Global Economy: Mercantile Empires and Worldwide Trade
    1.   Colonial Empires
    2.   Global Trade

IV.   The Social Order of the Eighteenth Century
    A.   The Peasants
    B.   The Nobility
    C.   The Inhabitants of Towns and Cities

Chapter Summary:

While Europe experienced the scientific and intellectual revolutions of the seventeenth and eighteenth centuries, its various states moved from early modern absolutism to the verge of republican revolution. Across the continent the Old Regimes experienced the last set of crises in what can now be seen as preparation for the convulsions that ushered in the modern age.

It was a time of what has been called "enlightened absolutism," although how enlightened the rulers were depends on the nation being studied. In Britain and Holland, kingship gave way to representative government, even if those being represented were the upper classes, while in France and eastern Europe, various forms of absolutism continued. In Prussia, for example, the Hohenzollerns gave their people efficiency and military glory without granting them civil rights, while in Austria the Emperor Joseph II tried to make liberal philosophy his lawmaker, but in the end believed he had failed.

Warfare became much more efficient during the eighteenth century, and wars defined the future even more than they had in the century before. Prussia took its place in the ranks of the strong nation-states with its successes in the War of the Austrian Succession. Britain won the war for overseas empire with its victory over France in the Seven Years' War.

Meanwhile, populations continued to grow, and improvements in agriculture production and the riches of overseas colonies increased national prosperity in most countries. However, the gap between rich and poor grew ever more pronounced, and poverty virtually overwhelmed organizations and governments that tried to do something to remedy it. The stage was set for social revolution and the military strife that usually follows it.

Identify:

1.   Natural rights   [p. 363]

2.   United Kingdom   [p. 364]

3.   Pocket borough   [p. 364]

4.   Hanoverians   [p. 365]

5.   Robert Walpole   [p. 365]

6.   Junkers   [pp. 366-367]

7.   Joseph II   [pp. 368-369]

8.   Catherine II   [p. 369]

9.   Emelyan Pugachev   [p. 369]

10.   Robert Clive   [pp. 371-372]

11.   Plains of Abraham   [pp. 372-373]

12.   Cottage industry   [p. 375]

Match the following words with their definitions:

1.	Marie Antoinette	A.	Austrian ruler who led political and fiscal reforms
2.	Robert Walpole	B.	sought to make "Philosophy" Austria's Lawmaker
3.	William Pitt the Elder	C.	won India for Britain
4.	Junkers	D.	frivolous Austrian wife of French King Louis XVI
5.	Maria Theresa	E.	a cause of the Seven Years War
6.	Joseph II	F.	died winning Quebec
7.	Silesia	G.	member of the Prussian ruling class
8.	Robert Clive	H.	lost Quebec and his life
9.	James Wolf	I.	British prime minister whom George I and II permitted to run their governments
10.	Louis-Joseph Montcalm	J.	British Prime Minister whose government won Canada

Multiple-Choice:

1. France in the eighteenth century

    a. prospered under the enlightened philosophe Louis XV.
    b. suffered severe economic depression throughout the century.
    c. was torn apart by civil wars.
    d. lost an empire and acquired a huge public debt.

2. Political developments in eighteenth-century Britain included

    a. Parliament taking over the last remaining powers of the monarchy.
    b. the rearranging of boroughs to make elections to the Commons more fair.
    c. calls for reform after the corrupt Prime Ministry of Pitt the Younger.
    d. the increasing influence and power of the king's ministers to make public policy.

3.   A continuing trend through the eighteenth century in Prussia was

   a.   that the bureaucracy was out of control.
   b.   the social and military dominance of the Junkers.
   c.   a reluctance to get involved in European wars.
   d.   social mobility for peasants through civil service.

4.   Frederick the Great of Prussia succeeded in

   a.   imposing his strict Protestantism on his populace.
   b.   crushing the power of the Prussian nobility.
   c.   carrying out all the philosophes' calls for reform.
   d.   creating greater unity for Prussia's scattered lands.

5.   Joseph II's reforms included all of the following *except*

   a.   complete religious toleration.
   b.   the abolition of serfdom.
   c.   the construction of internal trade barriers.
   d.   establishment of the principle of equality of all before the law.

6.   Russia's Catherine the Great

   a.   followed successfully a policy of expansion against the Turks.
   b.   instigated enlightened reforms for the peasantry after the Pugachev revolt.
   c.   alienated the nobility with her extensive enlightened reforms.
   d.   had two of her sons assassinated to prevent their further plotting against her.

7.   Enlightened absolutism in the eighteenth century

   a.   never completely overcame the political and social realities of the day.
   b.   was most successful in strengthening administrative systems in the nation-states.
   c.   was limited to policies that did not undermine the interests of the nobility.
   d.   all of the above

8.   European warfare in the eighteenth century was characterized by

   a.   reliance on mercenary armies on the continent.
   b.   ideological fervor that led to bloody battles.
   c.   using standing armies to settle political disputes.
   d.   reluctance on the part of monarchs to fight against each other.

9.   Which of the following statements best applies to Europe's social order in the eighteenth century?

    a.   It differed from the Middle Ages in that wealth was the sole determining factor in a person's social standing.

    b.   The nobility was homogeneous and served the same social function throughout Europe.

    (c.) Peasants were still hindered by a variety of feudal services and fees imposed by powerful nobles.

    d.   Peasants and nobles grew closer socially in eastern Europe, where serfdom was eradicated.

10.   The eighteenth century European nobility

    (a.) played a large role in administering nation-states.

    b.   lost its old dominance in military affairs.

    c.   composed twenty percent of Europe's population.

    d.   differed little in wealth and power from state to state.

Complete the following sentences:

1.   Because several seats in the British Parliament could be controlled by one man—seats from what were called _____ boroughs—the House of Commons was dominated by the _____ aristocracy.

2.   William Pitt the Younger served King _____ ____ through the times of the _____ Revolution and the wars of _____.

3.   Frederick the Great of Prussia proved to be an enlightened ruler by granting his people limited freedom of _____ and the _____ and complete religious _____.

4.   When Joseph II of Austria succeeded his mother _____ _____ as sole ruler, he announced that _____ was to be the lawmaker of his empire.

5.   The peasants' revolt against Catherine the Great of Russia was led by the Cossack _____ _____, who was finally captured and _____, after which Catherine halted all _____ reforms.

6.   Frederick II of Prussia used the succession of a _____ to the throne of Austria to invade _____ and plunge Europe into the War of the _____ _____.

7.   Outside Europe the Seven Years' War was fought in _____ and _____ _____ to see whether Britain or France would have the greater _____.

8.   On the Plains of _____ both the British General _____ and the French General _____ were killed. At the end of the Seven Years' War, North America belonged to _____.

9.   The most important European products of the eighteenth century were _____, which were made both in city _____ _____ and in rural _____ _____.

10.   European nations sought colonies in the West Indies to provide them with tobacco, _____, _____, and _____, all raised by _____ labor.

Place the following in chronological order and give dates:

1.   Joseph II begins his sole rule in Austria   1.

2.   The Seven Years' War   2.

3.   The Hanoverian Succession in Britain   3.

4.   Pugachev Rebellion in Russia   4.

5.   Third Partition of Poland   5.

6.   Frederick the Great begins reign in Prussia   6.

7.   William Pitt the Younger becomes Prime Minister   7.

Questions for Critical Thought: In each essay, fully explore the topic by answering the questions that follow it.

1.   "Enlightened Despotism." What three important rulers of the eighteenth century considered themselves enlightened? What did each do to prove the point? How do they rank in order of success?

2.   Limited Monarchy in Britain. How did Britain arrive at a system of governance in which the monarch was limited in power? What individuals and events made this development possible? Why didn't the same process occur in France? What were the consequences for each country?

3.   War and Diplomacy in the Eighteenth Century. How did diplomacy and the conduct of war in the eighteenth century differ from those of earlier times? How did the War of the Austrian Succession and the Seven Years' War illustrate eighteenth century diplomacy and warfare? How did each war affect Europe's future?

4.   Economy and Society in the Eighteenth Century. How did lives of the aristocracy and peasants differ in this era? What effects did agricultural production have on each group? How did the ripening colonial empires affect each?

Analysis of Primary Source Documents:

1.   After reading the correspondence between Frederick of Prussia and his father, how would you think he probably described "the old man" to friends his own age? What predictions would an objective reader have made about Frederick's future as a king?

2.   What does Clive's letter describing the battle at Plassey say about the temperament of an eighteenth century British general? What does it say about why Britain won the wars for empire?

3.   What do contemporary descriptions of slave trading say about white attitudes toward blacks? To what degree did white men consider slaves humans?

4.   Describe a debate that might have occurred between an advocate of free market economy and one who believed in government programs to help the poor in eighteenth-century France.

19 A REVOLUTION IN POLITICS: THE ERA OF THE FRENCH REVOLUTION AND NAPOLEON

Chapter Outline:

I.   The Beginnings of the Revolutionary Age: The American Revolution
    A.   Reorganization, Resistance, and Rebellion
    B.   The War for American Independence
    C.   Toward a New Nation: The U.S. Constitution

II.   The French Revolution
    A.   Background
        1.   Class Grievances: the Three Estates
            a.   Privileges of the Clergy and Nobility
            b.   A Rising Middle Class Without Power
        2.   A Financial Emergency
        3.   The Calling of the Estates-General
        4.   The Formation of the National Assembly
        5.   The Storming of the Bastille
    B.   The Destruction of the Old Regime
        1.   Declaration of the Rights of Man and the Citizen
        2.   Civil Constitution of the Clergy
        3.   A Constitutional Monarchy
        4.   Attacks from Other Monarchies and War in Europe
    C.   The Radical Revolution
        1.   Proclamation of a Republic
        2.   Execution of Louis XVI
    D.   A Nation in Arms
    E.   The Committee of Public Safety, Robespierre, and a Reign of Terror
    F.   The "Republic of Virtue"
    G.   Reaction and the Directory

III.   The Age of Napoleon
   A.   His Rise to Power
        1.   Victories in Italy
        2.   Consulship (1799-1804)
        3.   Emperor (1804-1815)
   B.   His Domestic Policies
        1.   Concordat with the Church
        2.   The Code Napoleon
        3.   Centralization of Administration
   C.   His Grand Empire and the European Response
        1.   Spread of Revolutionary Principles
        2.   The Continental System
        3.   Fiasco in Russia
        4.   Elba and Return
        5.   Waterloo and St. Helena

Chapter Summary:

The late eighteenth century saw the coming of revolutions long overdue, revolutions that combined the ideals of the philosophes with the frustrations of social and economic groups long denied equal rights and powers in their nation-states. Europe, and indeed the world, was never the same again.

The revolution began, of all places, in the British colonies along the American east coast. Pushed to rebellion by a growing dissatisfaction with the way Britain administered their affairs for them, the colonists declared their independence and to the world's surprise, but not without the world's help, made good on their boasts. They tried with some success to establish a republic based on the theories of the Enlightenment. The example was not lost on Europeans.

Within a decade of America's independence, when Louis XVI of France called his Estates-General to help him raise revenues, the Third Estate declared itself a national Assembly and proceeded to initiate the French Revolution. Within four years France executed Louis XVI and formed a Republic. Through the rest of the century France led the way to a reordering of the Old Regime and incurred the wrath of all the kings of Europe. When the radical phase of the revolution went too far and France found herself beset with enemies on every side, a conservative reaction set in and led to the rise of the liberal dictator who made himself emperor of the French—Napoleon Bonaparte.

For a decade Napoleon remade the map of Europe, using his military genius to bring the liberal ideals of the revolution to the nations he conquered. Even after he was defeated and exiled, and after royal figures were restored to their thrones, the spirit of the French Revolution lived on to inspire succeeding generations. The world in which we live was born in these revolutions of the late eighteenth and early nineteenth centuries.

Identify:

1.   Second Continental Congress   [p. 384]

2.   Bill of Rights   [p. 386]

3.   Estates-General   [p. 387]

4.   Tennis Court Oath   [p. 388]

5.   Bastille   [pp. 388-389]

6.   Declaration of the Rights of Man   [pp. 389-391]

7.   Olympe de Gouges   [pp. 389-391]

8.   Civil Constitution of the Clergy   [pp. 391-392]

9.   Committee of Public Safety   [pp. 394-396]

10.   Reign of Terror   [pp. 394-397]

11.   Dechristianization   [pp. 395-396]

12.   Thermidorian Reaction   [p. 396]

13.   The Directory   [pp. 396-398]

14.   Concordat   [p. 396-398]

15.   Code Napoleon   [pp. 399-400]

16.   St. Helena   [p. 403]

Match the following words with their definitions:

1.	Stamp Act	A.	first step in the French Revolution
2.	Articles of Confederation	B.	instituted the Reign of Terror
3.	Tennis Court Oath	C.	the revolutionary name for Notre Dame Cathedral
4.	Bastille	D.	meant to raise revenues to pay for defending the British colonies
5.	Committee of Public Safety		
6.	Lyons	E.	site of naval battle that led Napoleon to adopt the Continental System
7.	Temple of Reason	F.	the month in which the French Revolution took a conservative turn
8.	Thermidor		
9.	Concordat	G.	Paris prison that became the symbol of royal oppression
10.	Trafalgar	H.	Nearly 2,000 of its citizens were executed in 1494.
		I.	Napoleon's agreement with the Catholic Church
		J.	the first American constitution

Multiple-Choice:

1. After 1763 British authorities and American colonists came into conflict over

   a. how to pay for defending the colonies.
   b. expansion west of the Mississippi.
   c. freedom of religious expression.
   d. treatment of French prisoners of war.

2. France aided the American colonists
   a. in support of liberal ideals.
   b. to gain fur trading rights along the Mississippi.
   c. in support of the Quebecois.
   d. to get revenge on Britain.

3.   The British were forced to surrender to the Americans largely because of

    a.   lack of support from the people of England.
    b.   the combined forces of Americans, French, and other European nations.
    c.   the military superiority of the Americans.
    d.   an outbreak of the Bubonic Plague in London that reduced the number of military volunteers.

4.   The United States Bill of Rights

    a.   were copied from the Articles of Confederation.
    b.   were viewed by European liberals as too utopian to last.
    c.   depended heavily on the political theories of French philosophes.
    d.   had little or no influence on the ensuing French Revolution.

5.   The immediate cause of the French Revolution was

    a.   military losses against Britain.
    b.   a series of financial reversals.
    c.   religious turmoil.
    d.   the ideas of the philosophes.

6.   The controversy over voting by order rather than voting by head in the Estates-General meeting led to

    a.   a motion by the Nobles of the Robe to adjourn.
    b.   a move by "lovers of liberty" to block voting by head.
    c.   the expulsion of the Third Estate.
    d.   the decision of the Third Estate to form a National Assembly.

7.   In the Reign of Terror's "preservation" of the revolution from its internal enemies

    a.   the nobility was singled out for total annihilation.
    b.   rebellious cities were brutally crushed by the army.
    c.   no more than 5,000 were killed at the guillotine.
    d.   the Committee of Public Safety played little part.

8.   The program of dechristianization did *not* include

    a.   a new secular calendar.
    b.   removal of saints' names from street signs.
    c.   a systematic execution of Catholic leaders.
    d.   changing the names of church buildings.

9.   Which of the following statements best applies to Napoleon's domestic policies?

    a.   Great autonomy was given to provincial administrations.
    b.   His "new aristocracy" was based on wealth birth.
    c.   His Civil Code reaffirmed the ideals of the Revolution while creating a uniform legal system.
    d.   He reestablished Catholicism as the official state religion.

10.   Napoleon's Continental System tried to defeat Britain by

    a.   a massive invasion across the English Channel.
    b.   preventing Britain from trading freely.
    c.   fomenting civil war in Scotland.
    d.   giving arms to the Irish Republican Army.

Complete the following sentences:

1.   Britain's first scheme to raise money for defense of its American lands, the
    _____ _____ of 1765, was quickly repealed, but tensions grew
    until the _____ Continental Congress declared independence from Britain.

2.   Because the American Bill of Rights had roots in the French philosophes' theory of
    _____ _____, many Europeans saw the American Revolution
    as a fulfillment of the political dreams of the _____.

3.   Hoping the Estates-General would help him avoid the collapse of French
    _____, Louis XVI called it into session at _____ in May, 1789,
    opening the way for the French _____.

4.   Under the Civil Constitution of the Clergy, bishops and priests were to be elected by the
    _____ and paid by the _____ and had to take an oath of
    allegiance to the _____ _____.

5. Under the Committee of Public Safety, courts were organized to protect the French Republic from _____ _____, and thousands died by the _____ in what came to be called the Reign of _____.

6. The movement of dechristianization removed the prefix _____ from street signs, changed the name of the Cathedral of _____ _____, and urged priests to _____.

7. Robespierre's radical attempt to create the Republic of _____ led to a reaction in the month of _____ and a new government called The _____.

8. Napoleon's Concordat with the Catholic Church permitted church _____ and the reopening of _____, and it declared the church no longer an _____ of the government.

9. Napoleon's Continental System was meant to weaken _____ economically and destroy her capacity to _____ _____. It failed to do so because other continental countries resented French economic _____.

10. After his first exile on _____, Napoleon returned to rule France until his defeat at _____ and final exile on _____ _____.

Place the following in chronological order and give dates:

1. Napoleon's Russian Fiasco   1.

2. Battle of Waterloo   2.

3. Continental System established   3.

4. Storming of the Bastille   4.

5. Declaration of American Independence   5.

6. The End of the Seven Years' War   6.

7. Execution of Louis XVI   7.

Questions for Critical Thought: In each essay, fully explore the topic by answering the questions that follow it.

1. The Outbreak of the French Revolution. What were the conditions in France just before the Revolution? What part did the class system play in the eruption? How did the economy contribute to it? How did a meeting of the Estates-General turn into a full-blown revolution?

2. The Radical Phase of the Revolution. Why did the Revolution turn radical? What led to the storming of the Bastille and eventually the execution of Louis XVI? Why did a government dedicated to "public safety" institute the Reign of Terror? What do all of these events tell us about the nature of revolutions?

3. The Emperor Napoleon. What was Napoleon's background? How was he able to rise to such great power? What philosophy motivated and guided him? Did he create the age named for him, or did the age create him? What were his lasting accomplishments?

4. The Empire of Napoleon. Why did France begin its wars of conquest that led to an empire? What part did Napoleon play in the story? How did Napoleon organize and run his empire? Why did it finally fall? What effects did it have on the formation of the modern world?

Analysis of Primary Source Documents:

1. Describe the storming of the Bastille, and explain why this bloody event came to symbolize the French "triumph of justice and liberty."

2. What does the Declaration of the Rights of Man and the Citizen say about what the French revolutionaries were trying to destroy and what they were trying to create? How is the Declaration liberal, and how is it conservative?

3. Use Anne-Félicité Guinée's experience with the justice system during the Reign of Terror to show the insecurity of the regime that sought to make France a democracy.

4. Pick out the words (nouns, adjectives, verbs) Napoleon used in his addresses to create images and emotions that would inspire courage and determination in his men.

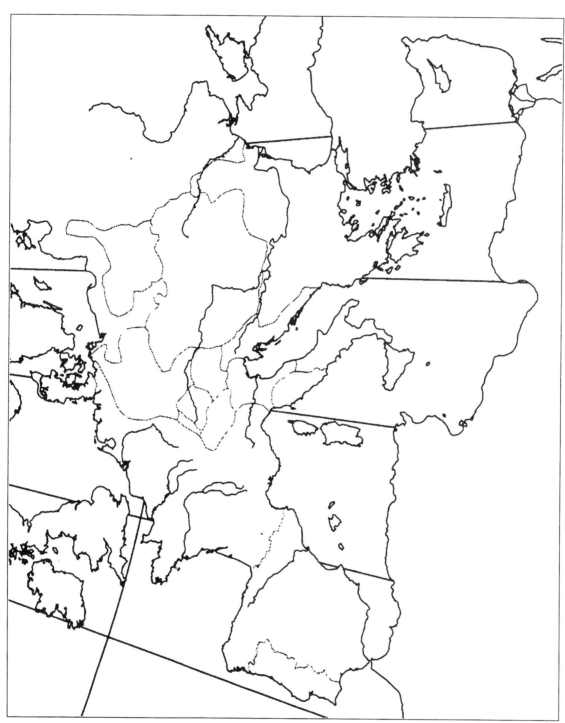

Map Exercise 11

Map Exercise 11: Napoleon's Empire

Using various colors of pencil, shade and label the following:

1. Austrian Empire
2. Bavaria
3. Britain
4. Confederation of the Rhine
5. Corsica
6. Denmark
7. France
8. Grand Duchy of Warsaw
9. Kingdom of Naples
10. Kingdom of Sicily
11. Prussia
12. Spain
13. Sweden
14. Switzerland

Pinpoint and label the following:

1. Auerstädt
2. Austerlitz
3. Berlin
4. Borodino
5. Brussels
6. Copenhagen
7. Danzig
8. Jena
9. Kiev
10. Madrid
11. Marseilles
12. Milan
13. Moscow
14. Paris
15. Trafalgar
16. Ulm
17. Vienna
18. Warsaw
19. Waterloo

20 THE INDUSTRIAL REVOLUTION AND ITS IMPACT ON EUROPEAN SOCIETY

Chapter Outline:

I. The Industrial Revolution in Great Britain
    A. Its Origins and Causes
        1. Capital for Investment
        2. Mineral Resources
        3. Ready Markets
    B. Technological Changes and New Forms of Industrial Organization
        1. The Cotton Industry's Power Looms
        2. James Watt's Steam Engine
        3. The Iron Industry
        4. Railroads: A Revolution in Transportation
            a. Richard Trevithick's Locomotive
            b. George Stephenson's *Rocket*
        5. The Industrial Factory
    C. The Great Exhibition: Britain in 1851

II. The Spread of Industrialism
    A. Industrialism on the Continent
        1. Technical Education
        2. Government Support
    B. The Industrial Revolution in the United States
        1. Internal Transportation
        2. Labor Supply

III. The Social Impact of the Industrial Revolution
    A. Population Growth
        1. Decline in Famine
        2. The Irish Famine
    B. Growth of Cities
        1. Urban Living Conditions
        2. The Chadwick Report

Chapter Summary:

The Industrial Revolution that came first to Britain and then to the continent of Europe changed the political and social order of Western people fully as much as the religious revolution called the Reformation, the intellectual revolution of the Enlightenment, or the political revolutions that followed the French Revolution. It changed the lives of the common worker more than any of those revolutions.

The Industrial Revolution started in Britain, where inventions, organizational skills, and natural resources combined to remake the countryside and the cities. It spread after a generation to the continent, particularly to places that had the same natural resources and organizational systems as Britain, and by the middle of the nineteenth century was redefining society throughout the Western world. The Great Exhibition of 1851 in London demonstrated the achievements, but did not point out the human suffering that accompanied those achievements.

The social impact of the Industrial Revolution is still being observed and assessed. A tremendous growth in city populations, the creation of a new middle class and a working class, and an ever increasing gap in earnings and quality of life between owners and workers, all helped to make the modern age what it has been for a century—for better and for worse. The most striking losers in this new age were for many decades the children who were literally "used up" to supply labor for factories.

Eventually reaction came. The workers themselves, however limited their powers might be, began calling for more rights to determine their work and lives; social reformers made the case of the workers so articulately that at last governments had to respond. The class struggle of modern times was underway.

Identify:

1.   Edmund Cartwright   [p. 408]

2.   James Watt   [p. 408]

3.   Henry Cort   [p. 409]

4.   Richard Trevithick   [p. 409]

5.   George Stevenson   [p. 409]

6.   Crystal Palace   [pp. 410-411]

7.   Harpers Ferry   [pp. 413-414]

8.   Irish Famine   [pp. 415-416]

9.   Edwin Chadwick   [p. 417]

10.   Factory Acts   [pp. 420-421]

11.   Luddites   [p. 421]

12.   Chartism   [p. 421]

Match the following words with their definitions:

1.   Edmund Cartwright   A.   site of the Great Exhibition of 1851

2.   James Watt   B.   attacked machines that threatened their livelihood

3.   George Stephenson   C.   lawyer who championed the cause of the urban poor

4.   Crystal Palace   D.   inventor of the power weaving loom

5.   Harpers Ferry   E.   inventor of the steam engine

6.   Edwin Chadwick   F.   where muskets with interchangeable parts were made

7.   Factory Acts   G.   limited the work hours of women and children

8.   Luddites   H.   His *Rocket* was the first locomotive used on a public
                                   railway line.
9.   Chartists
                              I.   demanded universal male suffrage
10. Coal Mines Act
                              J.   forbade employing boys under age of ten

Multiple-Choice:

1.   Britain led the way in the Industrial Revolution because it had a

     a.   pool of surplus labor ready to work.
     b.   central bank that offered flexible credit.
     c.   system of efficient transportation.
     d.   all of the above

2.   In the eighteenth century Britain's cotton industry

     a.   could not keep pace with French textile production.
     b.   was responsible for creating the first modern factories.
     c.   declined due to the lack of technical innovations.
     d.   went bankrupt due to gains in synthetic fiber production.

3.   The Great Exhibition of 1851

   a.   showed how the Industrial Revolution had achieved human domination over nature.
   b.   displayed Britain's industrial wealth and might to the world.
   c.   was housed in the Crystal Palace, itself a tribute to British engineering skills.
   d.   all of the above.

4.   The Industrial Revolution in the United States

   a.   never matched Britain's due to the lack of a system of internal transportation.
   b.   employed large numbers of women in factories, especially in textile mills.
   c.   utilized a labor-intensive system with many skilled workers.
   d.   was limited mainly to the southern states.

5.   The European population explosion of the nineteenth century

   a.   can be explained by increased birthrates.
   b.   was largely caused by the disappearance of famine.
   c.   was due to the absence of emigration.
   d.   occurred despite the return of major epidemic diseases.

6.   Which of the following statements best applies to urban life in the early nineteenth century in Europe?

   a.   Government intervention prevented consumer fraud and food contamination.
   b.   The decline in death rates accounted for increased populations in most large cities.
   c.   Lower-class family dwellings were on the whole much nicer than those in the country side.
   d.   Filthy sanitary conditions were exacerbated by the refusal of city authorities to take responsibility.

7.   In 1842 Edwin Chadwick published a landmark study of British

   a.   poverty and urged greater sanitation.
   b.   industrial profits and urged more mercantilism.
   c.   schools and urged more instruction in ethics.
   d.   fires and urged asbestos housing.

8.   The use of children in the workplace during the early Industrial Revolution

    a.   toughened and strengthened them physically for their adult lives.
    b.   continued the pre-industrial practice of working children hard.
    c.   did not occur in mining operations, where children were never used because they were too small.
    d.   was often prevented by parish officials who employed children as pauper apprentices only for clerical work.

9.   Before 1870 women's wages in textile mills were

    a.   the same as men's.
    b.   paid to their husbands.
    c.   half that of men's.
    d.   paid in foodstuffs.

10.   The Luddites

    a.   received little local support from the people in their areas of activities.
    b.   physically attacked machines they believed adversely affected their livelihood.
    c.   were the lowest of unskilled workers in Britain.
    d.   were the first movement of the working classes on the continent.

Complete the following sentences:

1.   Britain led the Industrial Revolution because it had deposits of _____ and _____, because it had abundant _____, and because of its small _____.

2.   The cotton industry was pushed forward dramatically by the spinning jenny of James _____ and the power loom of Edmund _____.

3.   Richard Trevithick pioneered the use of the steam-powered _____, but George Stephenson's _____ was the first used on a public line.

4.   The Great Exhibition of 1851, held in the _____ _____ in the London suburb of _____, demonstrated that _____ led the world in industry.

5.   On the continent, governments supported _____ education, awarded grants to _____, and even financed _____.

6.   In Ireland, where _____ peasants rented from absentee British
      _____ landlords, a mid-century _____ crop failure led to
      massive starvation.

7.   As secretary for the _____ _____ Commission, Edwin Chadwick
      blamed urban diseases on _____ impurities and called for reforms in
      _____.

8.   Children were extensively used in factories because of their small _____,
      because they were easily _____ to work, and because they were a
      _____ supply of labor.

9.   The aim of the People's Charter of 1838 was political _____ and so demanded
      universal _____ suffrage and _____ for service in Parliament.

10.   Between 1833 and 1897 reformers forced factories to limit the workday of small children to
      _____ hours and all children between thirteen and eighteen to _____
      hours. Boys under ten were not permitted to work in _____.

Place the following in chronological order and give dates:

1.   The Great Exhibition   1.

2.   People's Charter written   2.

3.   Cartwright invents the power loom   3.

4.   Watt invents the rotary steam engine   4.

5.   Ten Hours Act   5.

6.   Trevithick first uses the steam locomotive   6.

7.   Luddites attack machines   7.

Questions for Critical Thought: In each essay, fully explore the topic by answering the questions

Questions for Critical Thought: In each essay, fully explore the topic by answering the questions that follow it.

1.   The Industrial Revolution in Britain. What conditions were needed for the industrial revolution to take place, and why was Britain prepared to lead the way? What persons, inventions, and discoveries helped start and perpetuate this revolution on the island? How did the Great Exhibition of 1851 symbolize and demonstrate Britain's leadership role?

2.   The Spread of Industrialism. How did the industrial revolution on the continent differ from that in Britain? Why and how did the German lands eventually match and even surpass Britain in productivity? How was the revolution in the United States different from those in Britain and on the continent? What difficulties did the Americans face, and what factors favored eventual American superiority?

3.   The Social Impact of the Industrial Revolution. How did the revolution affect the lives of working people? How did it affect the lives of the rising middle class? What were the results of the economic gap between the classes that developed during the industrial revolution?

4.   Responses to the Industrial Revolution. How did the industrial system abuse working class people? Why did they seek to create trade unions, and how successful were they in doing so? What roles did the Luddites and the Chartists play in the attempt to redress grievances? What did the British Parliament do to end abuses? What more could it have done?

Analysis of Primary Source Documents:

1.   List the traits Edward Baines said made Richard Arkwright a successful entrepreneur. Then list conditions, advantages, and probable personal traits that Baines failed to mention, but which hindsight tells us also helped.

2.   Describe the likely appearance and personality of a man or woman who had worked for five years under the rules of the Berlin Trading Company.

3.   What almost-hidden commentary about American life as industrialism grew was Mark Twain making when he described the arrival of a steamboat?

4.   What would you, a reform minded member of the British Parliament, have recommended the government do about child labor abuse? What would you have recommended as punishment for sadistic overseers?

CHAPTER

21 REACTION, REVOLUTION, AND ROMANTICISM, 1815-1850

Chapter Outline:

I. The Conservative Order, 1815-1830
  A. The Conservative Domination: The Concert of Europe
    1. Edmund Burke's *Reflections* as Guide
    2. Intervention by the Great Powers
  B. Revolt in Latin America
  C. The Greek Revolt, 1821-1832
  D. The Conservative Domination: The European States
    1. Rule of the Tories in Britain
    2. The Bourbon Restoration in France
      a. Louis XVIII's Moderation
      b. Charles X and the Revolt of 1830
    3. Intervention by the Powers in Italy
    4. Repression of Liberalism in Central Europe
    5. Tsarist Autocracy in Russia

II. The Ideologies of Change
  A. Liberalism: John Stuart Mill
  B. Nationalism
  C. Early Socialism: Robert Owen

III. Revolution and Reform, 1830-1850
  A. The Revolutions of 1830
    1. The July Revolt in France: A Bourgeois Monarchy
    2. Reform in Britain
  B. The Revolutions of 1848
    1. Yet Another French Revolution: a Second Republic, a Second Bonaparte
    2. Revolution in Central Europe
    3. Revolts in the Italian States
  C. The Growth of the United States

IV.   Culture in an Age of Reaction and Revolution: The Mood of Romanticism
    A.   Characteristics of Romanticism
        1.   Sentiment and the Inner World: The Example of Goethe
        2.   Individualism
        3.   The Lure of the Middle Ages
        4.   An Attraction to the Bizarre
    B.   Romantic Poets and the Love of Nature
        1.   Percy Bysshe Shelley
        2.   Lord Byron
        3.   William Wordsworth
    C.   Romanticism in Art and Music
        1.   Casper David Friedrich
        2.   Eugène Delacroix
        3.   Ludwig van Beethoven

Chapter Summary:

The Congress of Vienna, which made peace at the end of the Napoleonic Wars, tried to restore the Old Order and its "legitimate" rulers. It tried to establish a conservative system, with a balance of power, that would give Europe peace as far as it could see into the future. It succeeded, in a way, and for a time.

The conservative system was installed, but beneath a tranquil surface the barely suppressed ideals of liberty continued to stir up both hope and trouble. When combined with a rising call for independence and unification in nations long dependent and divided, it became a powerful agent of revolt and reform. Greece and the countries of Latin America threw off foreign masters. Revolts simmered and erupted finally in Russia, France, Austria, Germany, Belgium, Poland, and Italy. Some of them were successful, some were not, but together they made the first half of the nineteenth century a volatile time.

Intellectuals responded to the spirit of the times with various theories about human society. Men like Edmund Burke defended conservatism as the best system to preserve the institution that give people order and security. Some welcomed the continent-wide revolts of 1848, while some feared that political disintegration would soon follow, and perhaps both were surprised when the revolts led to more conservative regimes almost everywhere.

Across Europe dreamers sought freedom and a better way of life. Young people joined organizations dedicated to freeing their nations from foreign domination or uniting their separated peoples into new nations. Utopian socialists experimented with industrial and educational reforms. The cultural form of this mixed age of reaction and rebellion was Romanticism. Writers such as Geothe, Byron, and Wordsworth heralded individualism and glorified nature. The painter Delacroix and the composer Beethoven brought to the arts their age's suppressed urge to be free. It was a time brimming with emotion.

Romanticism - individualism
            - glorification of nature.

Identify:

1.   Metternich   [p. 424]

2.   Edmund Burke   [p. 425]

3.   Simón Bolívar   [p. 427]

4.   Tories and Whigs   [p. 428]

5.   Alexander I   [p. 429]

6.   Nicholas I   [p. 429]

7.   Louis-Philippe   [pp. 433-434]

8.   Charles Louis Napoleon Bonaparte   [p. 434]

9.   Louis Kossuth   [pp. 434-436]

10.   Giuseppe Mazzini   [p. 436]

11.   Romanticism   [pp. 438-441]

12.   Goethe   [p. 438]

13.   Eugene Delacroix   [p. 440]

14.   Beethoven   [pp. 440-441]

Match the following words with their definitions:

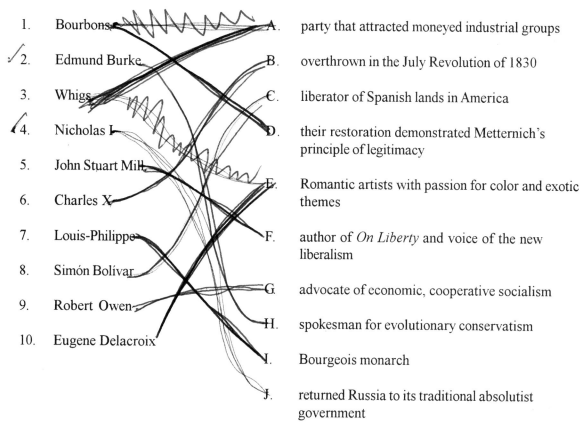

1. Bourbons
2. Edmund Burke
3. Whigs
4. Nicholas I
5. John Stuart Mill
6. Charles X
7. Louis-Philippe
8. Simón Bolívar
9. Robert Owen
10. Eugene Delacroix

A. party that attracted moneyed industrial groups

B. overthrown in the July Revolution of 1830

C. liberator of Spanish lands in America

D. their restoration demonstrated Metternich's principle of legitimacy

E. Romantic artists with passion for color and exotic themes

F. author of *On Liberty* and voice of the new liberalism

G. advocate of economic, cooperative socialism

H. spokesman for evolutionary conservatism

I. Bourgeois monarch

J. returned Russia to its traditional absolutist government

Multiple-Choice:

1. The Congress of Vienna

    a. gave Prussia complete control over Polish lands.
    b. sought to maintain a balance of power among members of the Quadruple Alliance.
    c. failed to achieve a long-lasting peace among the nations of Europe.
    d. treated France leniently, particularly after Napoleon's One Hundred Days.

2. Metternich

    a. supported the revolutionary ideology of the French philosophes.
    b. believed that a free press was necessary to maintain personal liberties.
    c. tried to restore monarchs who would uphold traditional values.
    d. was an atheist who supported the suppression of religion.

3.   Conservatism, which was the dominant political philosophy of Europe following the fall of Napoleon, was

      a.   rejected at Vienna by Metternich because it was inappropriate for the post-Napoleonic age.
      b.   careful to protect the rights of the individual.
      c.   best expressed intellectually by Edmund Burke in his *Reflections on the Revolution in France*.
      d.   too radical for the liberal Joseph de Maistre, an evolutionary socialist.

4.   The Concert of Europe was most successful at

      a.   ending the political domination of Greece by the Holy Alliance.
      b.   thwarting Britain's attempts to intervene and crush revolts in Italy and Spain.
      c.   crushing the colonial revolts in Latin America.
      d.   none of the above

5.   Political reforms in Britain in the 1830s included

      a.   relief for the unemployed through the Poor Law of 1834.
      b.   the granting of the vote to the lower industrial working class with the Reform Bill of 1832.
      c.   the repeal of the Corn Law in 1836, which increased the price of bread for workers.
      d.   granting suffrage to an upper middle class elite.

6.   The 1848 revolution in France resulted in

      a.   the continuation of Louis-Philippe's rule when he accepted liberal reforms.
      b.   new elections for the National Assembly, resulting in a victory for radical republicans.
      c.   Europe's first socialist state under the guidance of the workshops.
      d.   an authoritarian government ruled by President Louis Napoleon.

7.   The student response in Germany to the French Revolution of 1848 was one of

      a.   outrage and calls for war against France.
      b.   disbelief and despair over the coming chaos.
      c.   enthusiasm and hope that republican reforms would also come to Germany.
      d.   joy that the French state was about to self-destruct.

8.   The social and political upheavals in central Europe through 1848-1849 led to

    a.   the failure of the Frankfurt Assembly in Germany.
    b.   an independent state for Hungary.
    c.   a united German-Austrian state patterned on the dreams of the *Grossdeutsch*.
    d.   the continued dominance of Metternich in Austria.

9.   The Age of Romanticism was characterized by

    a.   Chateaubriand, whose paintings anticipated the Impressionist movement.
    b.   Beethoven, whose classical compositions gradually gave way to works of deep emotion.
    c.   Delacroix, who broke classical conventions by using only black and white in his paintings.
    d.   Friedrich, whose "program" music played on the emotions of listeners.

10.   The Age of Romanticism witnessed

    a.   a love of and nostalgia for medieval architecture.
    b.   rejection by artists and musicians of all religious sensibilities.
    c.   a decline in the number of Protestants in Britain.
    d.   the importation of Indian mysticism to Europe.

Complete the following sentences:

1.   At the Congress of Vienna, Austria was represented by Prince _Metternich_, who said he was guided by the principle of _legitimacy_, which meant rule by _Bourbon_ in France and Spain.

2.   The Napoleonic Era in Europe weakened Spanish control of the American colonies, and _Simon_ _Bolivar_, known as the Liberator, led Latin American armies of independence to victory. He was succeeded and his work was finished by _Jose_ _de_ _San_ _Martin_.

3.   By the Treaty of Adrianople, Turkey agreed to let _Russia_, _France_, and _Britain_ decide the fate of Greece. They declared her _independent_.

4.   After a _military_ _revolt_ against his accession, Russia's Nicholas I created a _secret_ _police_ organization to maintain order.

5. In his book _On Liberty_, John Stuart Mill described in eloquent language why the best society guarantees _liberty_ of the _individual_.

6. Robert Owen, a British _Cotton_ manufacturer, established cooperative communities at _New Lanark_ in Scotland and _New Harmony_ in Indiana.

7. The Revolutions of 1830 saw the emergence of a _Bourgeois_ monarchy in France and a new _Dutch_ Republic.

8. The French Revolution of 1848 deposed King _Louis_ – _Phillipe_ and established a Second Republic under President _Charles Louis Napoleon Bonaparte_.

9. Giuseppe Mazzini's nationalist organization _Young Italy_ put its hopes in the hands of _Charles Albert_, King of Piedmont. This king's one attempt to unify Italy, however, failed when he lost to the _Austrians_ in _Lombardy_.

10. Romantic literature featured a range of subjects, from the tragedies of the German _Goethe_, to the historical novels of the Scotsman _Walter Scott_, to strange tales such as _Frankenstein_ by _Mary Shelley_.

Place the following in chronological order and give dates:

1. Burke's _Reflections_ written   1.

2. Nicholas I begins reign in Russia   2.

3. July Revolution in France   3.

4. Greek royal dynasty established   4.

5. First British Reform Act   5.

6. Revolts or revolutions in France, Germany, Italy, and Austria   6.

7. Beginning of Wars of Independence in Latin America   7.

Questions for Critical Thought: In each essay, fully explore the topic by answering the questions that follow it.

1. The Congress of Vienna. What was the purpose of this meeting? Who represented which nations? What agreement did they work out? What did they mean by the term "balance of power"? Why is the achievement of the Congress called a Monument to Conservatism?

2. Conservatism and Liberalism in the Nineteenth Century. What is Conservatism, according to Edmund Burke and the leaders who considered themselves conservatives? What is Liberalism, according to John Stuart Mill and the leaders who considered themselves liberals? What were the goals of each group in the nineteenth century? What were each group's achievements?

3. The Year 1848. What were the major events of this year across Europe? How did those events affect the national identities of France, Italy, and Germany? What were the short- and long-term affects of this fateful year on European affairs?

4. Romanticism. What were the main characteristics of the Romantic Movement? Who were its leading figures? What did they achieve? How did the movement affect art, music, and social reform? What has Romanticism given to the modern world?

Analysis of Primary Source Documents:

1. According to Austria's Prince Metternich, what are the national characteristics that give a country security and stability? How does each characteristic contribute to the whole?

2. How did John Stuart Mill's views on "liberty" challenge the conservative establishment of his day? What does Mill consider the highest good in a society? What kind of a society comes about when this highest good is pursued?

3. Describe the enthusiasm of young German liberals like Carl Schurz when their long-awaited revolution seemed at hand. Suggest three probable reactions among such young men when they realized it had failed.

4. Explain the nineteenth century's love for "Gothic" literature, particularly its tendency to combine romance and horror, as illustrated by the writings of Edgar Allen Poe. What does this say about the age, and about the Romantic Movement?

22 AN AGE OF NATIONALISM AND REALISM, 1850-1871

Chapter Outline:

IV.   Industrialization and the Marxist Response
    A.   Prosperity and Trade
    B.   Marx and Marxism
        1.   The Life and Experience of Karl Marx
        2.   *The Communist Manifesto* and *Capital*
        3.   The First International

V.   Science and Culture in an Age of Realism
    A.   A New Age of Science
        1.   Proliferation of Discoveries
        2.   Faith in Science's Benefits
    B.   Darwin and Organic Evolution
    C.   Realism in Literature and Art
        1.   The Realistic Novel
            a.   Gustave Flaubert
            b.   William Thackeray
            c.   Charles Dickens
        2.   Realism in Art
            a.   Gustave Courbet
            b.   Jean-Francois Millet

Chapter Summary:

Just after the midpoint of the nineteenth century, the suppressed emotions that had constantly bubbled for three decades finally erupted. The nations of Europe spent their energies in unification or reform, and the results affected Western development for the next century.

The memories of Napoleonic greatness that had haunted France saw fulfillment with first the election as president and then the proclamation as emperor of Napoleon's nephew, who took the grand title Emperor Napoleon III. From 1852, until he was deposed following France's defeat by Prussia in 1870, Napoleon made and unmade policy across the continent and even meddled in the affairs of the New World. The dreams of Mazzini were fulfilled when Cavour and Garibaldi, working sometimes at odds, succeeded in unifying Italy for the first time since the fall of the Roman Empire. Under the guidance of Bismarck, Prussia maneuvered and fought its way, using the arts of *realpolitik*, to the head of a unified German Empire. In Russia and the United States, serfs and slaves were freed, in the former by imperial decree, in the latter by war and constitutional amendment. In Britain the pressures of industrialization led to reforms that made the realm of Queen Victoria more democratic.

Science continued to make discoveries and to change life both socially and personally. Yet, while health care greatly improved with discoveries about bacteria and infection, more and more workers fell into what Marx called the "wage slavery" of the industrial market. While political leaders like Disraeli and Gladstone believed that justice could be achieved by reform, Marx held that only a revolution of the workers would bring about a classless society. Both the *realpolitik* of nations and the realities of industrial life affected the arts, ushering in a new era of Realism. Novelists such as Flaubert and Dickens and painters such as Courbet and Millet showed readers and observers a stark world, without glamour or fantasy. The world was often brutal and grim, and they portrayed it with pitiless accuracy.

Realism – brutal grim

Identify:

1.   Napoleon III   [pp. 444-445]

2.   Crimea   [p. 445]

3.   Victor Emmanuel II   [p. 446-447]

4.   Red Shirts   [p. 447]

5.   Bismarck   [pp. 447-449]

6.   *Realpolitik*   [p. 477]

7.   Francis Joseph   [p. 450]

8.   *Zemstvos*   [p. 454]

9.   Disraeli   [p. 454]

10.   Karl Marx   [pp. 456-458]

11.   *Das Kapital*   [p. 457]

12.   Louis Pasteur   [p. 458]

13.   Thackeray   [p. 459]

14.   Courbet   [pp. 460-461]

Match the following words with their definitions:

1. Camillo di Cavour

2. Giuseppe Garibaldi

3. Otto von Bismarck

4. Benjamin Disraeli

5. John Macdonald

6. Proletariat

7. Louis Pasteur

8. Michael Faraday

9. Charles Darwin

10. Gustave Flaubert

A. conservative British prime minister who passed the Reform Bill of 1867

B. advocate of organic evolution

C. agent of *realpolitik*

D. beneficiaries of Marx's communist revolution

E. Prime Minister of Piedmont who helped make Victor Emmanuel King of Italy

F. builder of the first generator of electricity

G. author of the realist novel *Madame Bovary*

H. military leader who added Sicily to the new Kingdom of Italy

I. chemist who pioneered in fermentation and bacteriology

J. apostle of Canadian unification

Multiple-Choice:

1. In establishing the Second Empire, Napoleon III

    a. received the overwhelming support of the people.
    b. granted the National Assembly stronger powers.
    c. rescinded universal male suffrage.
    d. cared little about public opinion.

2. Napoleon III used his personal popularity and France's economic prosperity to rebuild

    a. the National Assembly.
    b. Charlemagne's ancient capital of Aix-la-Chapelle.
    c. the French Catholic Church.
    d. the city of Paris.

3. Napoleon III entered the Crimean War because he was convinced that he had an international mission to

    a. champion movements for national independence.
    b. conquer Europe for liberalism.
    c. arbitrate continental disputes.
    d. contain the military ambitions of Russia.

4. An overall result of the Crimean War was

    a. the reinforcement of the Concert of Europe until 1914.
    b. continued Russian expansionism into Europe for the next two decades.
    c. increased British involvement in continental affairs.
    d. an international climate in that both Italian and German unification were possible.

5. As leader of the Italian unification movement, Camillo di Cavour

    a. had no preconceived plan for the unification.
    b. personally led Italian troops against Austria.
    c. supported Prussia against Austria with Italian troops in 1866.
    d. used an alliance with the hated France to defeat Austria.

6. The immediate cause of the Franco-Prussian War was

    a. the ascent of a French prince to the Spanish throne.
    b. a Bismarck-edited telegram from King William I.
    c. the French invasion of Alsace-Lorraine.
    d. Napoleon III's annexation of Schleswig-Holstein.

7. The creation of the dual monarchy of Austria-Hungary

    a. allowed Magyars and German-speaking Austrians to dominate ethnic minorities.
    b. enabled Alexander von Bach to become an absolute dictator.
    c. left Hungary dependent in its foreign affairs.
    d. overturned the Compromise of 1867.

8. Russia and the United States were similar in the 1860's in that both

    a. experienced devastating civil wars.
    b. saw radical liberals assassinate high government officials.
    c. fought unsuccessful wars against Britain.
    d. emancipated enslaved populations within their borders.

9. According to Karl Marx's vision for the industrial future, the state would

    a. be violently destroyed with a class war.
    (b.) wither away because it would be unnecessary.
    c. dominate every part of the citizen's life.
    d. be made efficient through technological bureaucracy.

10. The second of Charles Darwin's books

    a. discussed plant and animal evolution.
    b. was a catalogue of his specimens in the British Museum.
    (c.) argued for the animal origins of humans.
    d. examined the Biblical theme of creation.

Complete the following sentences:

1. With the disintegration of the ___Ottoman___ Empire, Russia tried to carve out a new sphere of influence, only to be attacked in its ___Crimean___ Peninsula by France and ___Britain___, destroying the old ___Concert___ of Europe.

2. Garibaldi, who was above all a dedicated ___Italian___ ___Patriot___, was persuaded to accept an Italian kingdom under King ___Victor___ ___Emmanuel___ of the house of ___Savoy___.

3. In order to achieve German unification, Bismarck successfully went to war against ___Denmark___, ___Austria___, and ___France___, the latter ending with the proclamation of the German ___Empire___.

4. Alexander II's Emancipation Edict allowed former Russian serfs to own ___property___, to ___marry___ whom they chose, and to bring lawsuits, but resentment of his policies led to Alexander's ___assassination___ in 1881.

5. Although the British Liberal Party led in calls for voting reform, the Reform Bill of 1867 was passed under the leadership of the Conservative Prime Minister ___Disraeli___. In the next election, the ___Liberal___ Party won a huge victory.

6. John Macdonald, fearful of ___American___ plans to annex his country, pressured Britain into creating the ___Dominion___ of Canada, which was given self-rule in all matters except ___foreign___ ___affairs___.

7.   Marx and Engels claimed in their _Communist_ _Manifesto_ that a class war would end with the complete victory of the _proletariat_ over the _bourgeoisie_ and a _classless_ society.

8.   In his first book Charles Darwin described the evolution of only _plants_ and _animals_; however in a second book he discussed the *Descent of* _Man_ and concluded that humans have _animal_ origins.

9.   Flaubert's realist novel *Madame Bovary* tells of a provincial woman inspired by _romantic_ stories to experiment with _adultery_, only to end up a _suicide_, never repentant.

10. Courbet said he painted common people because he had never seen _angels_ or _goddesses_. His critics said he was leader of a cult of _ugliness_.

Place the following in chronological order and give dates:

1.   British Reform Act passed   1.

2.   American Civil War ends   2.

3.   Second Empire proclaimed in France   3.

4.   Italy annexes Rome   4.

5.   German Empire proclaimed   5.

6.   Austro-Prussian War   6.

7.   Russian Emancipation Edict   7.

Questions for Critical Thought: In each essay, fully explore the topic by answering the questions that follow it.

1.   The Second French Empire. What characteristics, personal and public, best describe Napoleon III? How was he able to establish the Second Empire? What did he accomplish during his eighteen years in power, both domestically and internationally? What were his greatest successes and greatest failures? How and why did the Empire end?

2. The Unification of Italy. Who were the major players in the drama of Italian unity and its eventual fulfillment? What were the obstacles to its realization, and how were they overcome? What circumstances conspired to achieve the dream of *risorgimento*?

3. The Unification of Germany. Who were the major players in the drama of German unity and its eventual fulfillment? What was Bismarck's role, and how did he use *realpolitik* to achieve his goals? What did German unification do to political equations of Europe?

4. The Age of Realism. What conditions led to the artistic and intellectual shift from Romanticism to Realism? What roles did the various scientists of the day play in this change? What kinds of literary and artistic works grew out of the new sensibility? How did Darwin and Marx fit into the picture? Should they be considered Romantics or Realists?

Analysis of Primary Source Documents:

1. Explain how Bismarck "edited" his king's telegram from Ems to make the French feel they had been insulted. How does this business demonstrate his *realpolitik*?

2. Compare and contrast the emancipation proclamations of Tsar Alexander II and Abraham Lincoln. Explain which was the more legally binding.

3. Having read Marx's description of the way we will arrive at the classless society, how would you judge Marx's opinion of human nature?

4. What made Charles Dickens' description of industrial Birmingham so powerful? What does his portrayal say about his own feelings on the subject?

Map Exercise 12

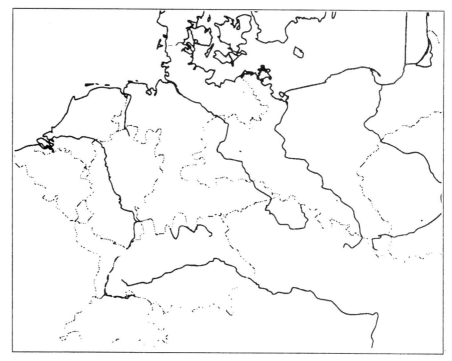

Map Exercise 12:   The Unification of Germany and Italy

Using various colors of pencil, shade and label the following:

Pinpoint and label the following:

Germany

1. Alsace
2. Baden
3. Bavaria
4. East Prussia
5. Hanover
6. Hesse
7. Lorraine
8. Oldenburg
9. Prussia
10. Schleswig-Holstein
11. West Prussia
12. Württemburg

Italy

1. Lombardy
2. Modena
3. Papal States
4. Parma
5. Piedmont
6. Romagna
7. Sardinia
8. Savoy
9. Tuscany
10. Two Sicilies
11. Umbria
12. Venezia

Germany

1. Berlin
2. Breslau
3. Frankfurt
4. Hamburg
5. Leipzig
6. Munich
7. Nuremburg
8. Strassburg
9. Trier
10. Weimar

Italy

1. Florence
2. Genoa
3. Milan
4. Naples
5. Rome
6. Venice

CHAPTER
23 MASS SOCIETY IN AN "AGE OF PROGRESS," 1871-1894

Chapter Outline:

I.   The Growth of Industrial Prosperity
    A.   New Products and New Markets
        1.   The Substitution of Steel for Iron
        2.   Electricity, the New Source of Energy
        3.   The Internal Combustion Engine
        4.   Consumer Products and Cartels
    B.   New Patterns in an Industrial Economy
        1.   From Depression to Prosperity
        2.   Economic Polarization
        3.   A World Economy
    C.   Women and New Job Opportunities
        1.   The Sweatshops
        2.   Office Work
    D.   Organizing the Working Class
        1.   Socialist Parties
        2.   Evolutionary Marxism
        3.   The Growth of Trade Unionism

II.   The Emergence of Mass Society
    A.   Population Growth
    B.   Transformation of the Urban Environment
        1.   The Growth of Cities
        2.   The Goals of Urban Reformers
            a.   Sanitation
            b.   Housing
    C.   The Social Structure of Mass Society
        1.   The Elite: Wealth and Status
        2.   The Middle Classes: Good Conduct
        3.   The Lower Classes: Skilled, Semiskilled, Unskilled

Chapter Summary:

After 1871, the nations of Europe were preoccupied for a quarter century with achieving true national unity, adjusting to the economics of a second industrial revolution, and adapting to the realities of rapid urbanization. Despite the rise and acceleration of international rivalries and animosities, the nations were simply too busy to fight among themselves.

During this period, inventions based on steel, electricity, and the internal combustion engine led to a new industrial economy, which changed the nature of markets and created a true world economy. Women found new opportunities for employment, yet also were seduced into a larger ring of subservience and prostitution. Socialist parties, with a more moderate form of Marxism, began organizing for action through trade unionism and political action. Europe suffered the birth pangs of a new age.

Mass society was born. The European population increased dramatically through better sanitation and diet, yet emigration prevented overcrowding. Class divisions continued to dictate styles of living, and women of the upper strata were encouraged to pursue a cult of domesticity, yet this age also saw the dawn of female consciousness and of birth control. The amount and quality of education increased in order to provide a better-trained work force and a more intelligent voting public, and there arose more opportunities to enjoy life through leisure activities. The European Nations moved in two opposite directions. In Britain and France, liberal parties increased democratic participation in government, while in Germany, Austria, and especially Russia, monarchs held to their powers with stubborn abandon. The times were changing, but it was not clear what the looming new century would bring.

Identify:

1.   "Day-Trippers" [p. 465]

2.   Cartels [p. 467] - formed to decrease competition internally.
    - independent enterprises worked together to control prices + fix products a quotas
    thereby restraining the kind of competition that led to reduced prices.

3.   August Bebel [pp. 469-470]
    - founder of the German Socialist Democratic Party.

4.   Eduard Bernstein [p. 470]
    - most prominent revisionist, argued in this book Evolutionary Socialism, evolution by
    democratic means, not revolution, would achieve the desired goal of socialism.

5.   Solomon Neumann [p. 473] (German) urban reformer.
    - blamed poor sanitation for epidemics.

6.   V. A. Huber [p. 474] - German housing reformer
    - to him good housing was a prerequisite for stable family life

7.   Consuelo Vanderbilt [p. 474]
    American who married into British royalty, brought her husband $10 million.

8.   Thomas Cook [p. 480]
    British pioneer of mass tourism
    responsible for organizing a railroad trip to temperance gathering in 1841.

9.   Rugby Union [p. 480]
    Rugby Football union formed in 1871.

10.   William Gladstone [p. 481]
    - passage of the Reform Act 1884
    - led the British Liberal party into a great age of reform.

11.   Paris Commune [pp. 481-482]
    radical republicans formed an independent republican government in Paris known
    as the commune   violently crushed in 1871.

12.   *Kulturkampf* [p. 483]
    launching an attack on the church (Catholic) "struggle for civilization"

13.   William II [p. 483] Emperor William II of Germany.
    - eager to pursue his own socialist politics

14.   Nicholas II [p. 484]

    when Alexander III died, his weak son + successor Nicholas II

    began his rule with his father's conviction that the absolute

    power of the tsars should be preserved.

Match the following words with their definitions:

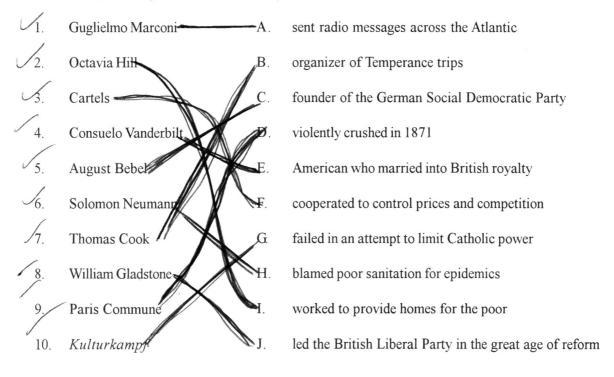

1. Guglielmo Marconi — A. sent radio messages across the Atlantic

2. Octavia Hill — B. organizer of Temperance trips

3. Cartels — C. founder of the German Social Democratic Party

4. Consuelo Vanderbilt — D. violently crushed in 1871

5. August Bebel — E. American who married into British royalty

6. Solomon Neumann — F. cooperated to control prices and competition

7. Thomas Cook — G. failed in an attempt to limit Catholic power

8. William Gladstone — H. blamed poor sanitation for epidemics

9. Paris Commune — I. worked to provide homes for the poor

10. *Kulturkampf* — J. led the British Liberal Party in the great age of reform

Multiple-Choice:

1. Cartels were designed primarily to

   a. enrich nation states.
   b. raise funds for social programs.
   c. restrain competition that lowers prices.
   d. provide police protection for companies.

2. Working-class men used which of these arguments to keep women out of industrial work?

   a. Keeping women at home made for stronger families.
   b. Women were physically too weak to do the work.
   c. It was not God's will for women to work.
   d. It would make women too politically active.

3.   Edward Bernstein stressed the need for

    a.   violent overthrow of capitalist governments.
    b.   extermination of individualists.
    c.   working within the political system to achieve socialism.
    d.   a literal faithfulness to every Marxist theory.

4.   The most successful legislative acts concerning public health

    a.   were passed in Russia.
    b.   created boards of health that fought for reforms.
    c.   seemed always to create more problems than they solved.
    d.   were condemned by church officials as socialistic.

5.   Octavia Hill's housing venture was designed to

    a.   give the poor an environment in which to improve themselves.
    b.   give charity to the helpless and hopeless poor.
    c.   let the wealthy experience poverty for a week each year.
    d.   break down class barriers.

6.   Experiments in public housing proved that

    a.   government housing was doomed to failure.
    b.   poor people would not keep their premises sanitary.
    c.   every project needed private monies to keep them afloat.
    d.   governments must construct houses on a grand scale.

7.   An example of the way new industrial wealth combined with old aristocracy was the marriage of the Duke of Marlborough to the

    a.   Italian Tia Ferrari.
    b.   American Wallis Warfield Simpson.
    c.   American Consuelo Vanderbilt.
    d.   German Bertha Krupp.

8.   The wealthy elite of the new industrial age

    a.   came to be dominated by upper-middle-class families with fortunes made in industry.
    b.   consisted mostly of landed aristocracy.
    c.   controlled only slightly more total wealth than did all the working class.
    d.   was more open to admission by newcomers in Russia than in any other country.

9.   The middle classes of late nineteenth-century Europe

~~a.~~   were composed of shopkeepers and manufacturers who barely lived above the property line.
b.   offered almost no opportunity for their women to improve themselves.
(c.)   were extremely concerned with propriety and adhered to values of hard work and Christian morality.
d.   viewed the idea of progress with extreme distrust.

10.   The Second French Empire was at last replaced by a

a.   restored monarchy, the "only true French regime."
b.   Third Empire, under Napoleon IV.
c.   Communist regime, allied with Soviet Russia.
(d.)   Third Republic, which survived despite internal divisions.

7/10

Complete the following sentences:

1.   In the late nineteenth century, Europe slowly divided into two zones, one _industrial_, the other _agricultural_, creating a massive economic _polarization_.

2.   Women first broke into the labor force because of the increased need for _white_ _collar_ workers. Most of the new jobs required few skills beyond basic literacy except for those in _teaching_ and _nursing_.

3.   Eduard Bernstein argued that Socialism was best achieved not by _revolution_, but by _evolution_. His approach can best be described as _socialism_.

4.   Between 1800 and 1900 London's population grew from _960,000_ to _6,500,000_ and Berlin's from _172,000_ to _2,700,000_.

5.   In England _London_ and _Liverpool_ were the first cities to have town councils build public housing, after concluding that _private_ _enterprise_ could not do all that was needed for the working classes.

6.   Even though vulcanized rubber made possible the manufacture of _condoms_ and _diaphragms_ by 1850, they were not widely used for birth control until the time of the First _World_ _War_.

7.   The chief motivation for providing mass education was _political_. It was used to teach _patriotism._, and it was believed that a common _language_ created national unity.

8.   The independent Parisian republic called the _Commune_ was ended when 20,000 people were _shot_ and 10,000 shipped to a _French_ penal _colony_.

9.   The _Prussian_ officers of the German army believed it their duty to defend the _monarchy_ and the _aristocracy_, and their general staff answered only to the _emperor_.

10.   The paranoid Russian Emperor Alexander III persecuted advocates of _Constitutional_ _reform monarchy_ and _social_ _reform_. He placed entire districts of his empire under _Nicholas II martial law_.

Place the following in chronological order and give dates:

1.   Bismarck's antisocialist law   1.

2.   Thomas Cook organizes his first tour   2.

3.   Reform Act passed by British Liberal Parliament   3.

4.   British Public Health Act   4.

5.   The Paris Commune   5.

6.   First human flight   6.

7.   First birth control clinic opened in Amsterdam   7.

Questions for Critical Thought: In each essay, fully explore the topic by answering the questions that follow it.

1.   The Second Industrial Revolution. How did the second phase of the industrial revolution differ from the first phase? What were the new sources of energy, the new products, and the new kinds of work after 1870? What political reactions did it provoke, especially among workers?

2.   The European Class System. How did industrialization and urbanization create a new class system? How did it differ from earlier systems? How did each group in it organize its life? How did women fit into the new system, both as family members and as workers?

3.   Life in an Age of Industry. What new social phenomena were born of the new age of industry? How did family structures adapt themselves to the new realities? Why and how did education for all become a centerpiece of national policy? What were the new forms of leisure, and how did they serve the needs of industrial society?

4.   Variety in Nineteenth Century European Nations. What kinds of government did various European nations have as the nineteenth century ended? How did each get to be that way? What obstacles and opportunities did each face, and how did each solve and take advantage of them? What did the new century offer each one?

Analysis of Primary Source Documents:

1.   Explain why department stores proved so successful. What needs did they satisfy, what did they offer the public, and what sound economic principles did they follow?

2.   Using Octavia Hill as your example, show how early reformers combined compassion for the poor with shrewd business sense.

3.   Give the response one of today's feminists might make to Elizabeth Poole Sanford's advice to women. (Use more than one word.)

4.   If you had been in Paris in 1871 and were writing an article about the events there for an American newspaper, how would you have explained it, particularly the motivations of people like Louise Michel?

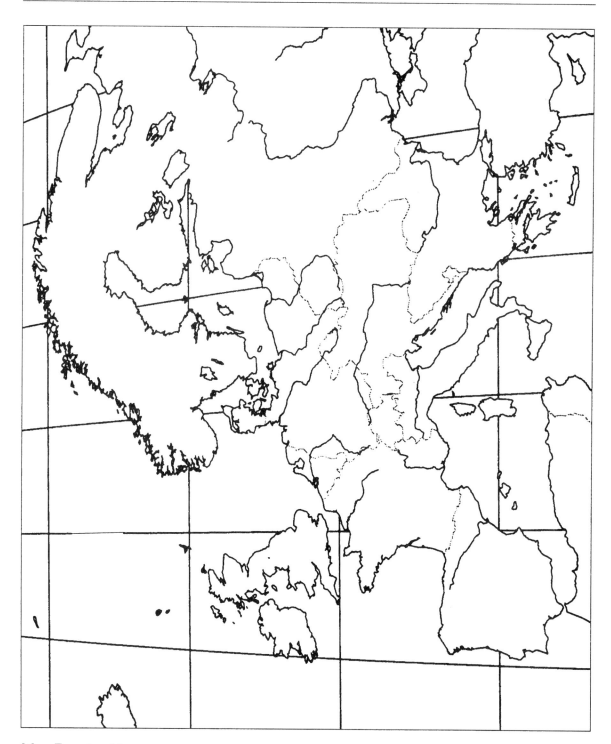

Map Exercise 13

Map Exercise 13:   Europe in 1871

Using various colors of pencil, shade and label where in Europe the following were found:

1.   Centers of population
2.   Coal
3.   Iron
4.   Oil

Label the following political divisions:

1.   Austrian Empire
2.   Belgium
3.   Britain
4.   France
5.   Italy
6.   Netherlands
7.   Norway
8.   Portugal
9.   Russia
10.   Spain
11.   Sweden
12.   Switzerland

CHAPTER
24 AN AGE OF MODERNITY AND ANXIETY, 1894-1914

Chapter Outline:

III. The New Imperialism
    A. Causes
        1. Competition among European Nations
        2. Social Darwinism and Racism
        3. Humanitarianism and Missions
        4. Economic Gain
    B. The Creation of Empires
        1. The Scramble for Africa
            a. Cape Colony and the Boer War
            b. Cecil Rhodes and British Strength
            c. Carving the Continent
        2. Asia in an Age of Imperialism
            a. James Cook and Australia
            b. China
            c. Matthew Perry and Japan
            d. The Pacific Islands
    C. Asian Responses to Imperialism

IV. International Rivalry and the Coming of War
    A. Bismarck's System of Alliances
    B. New Directions and New Crises: The Balkans

Chapter Summary:

The period from 1894 to 1914 saw Europe expand its horizons, both in the rise of daring, new intellectual and cultural developments at home and in the creation of new empires abroad.

At home, scientists were working on physical theories that would, in time, relegate the old Newtonian world to the past and usher in a much more insecure and dangerous world. Sigmund Freud concluded that man operates at the direction of unconscious motivations. The teachings of Charles Darwin were applied to society and used to justify racism and imperialism by saying that in the struggle of races and nations the fittest survive and make the world a better place. Christianity did constant battle with forces that threatened it. Modern forms began to appear in literature, the arts, and music, all of them rebellious against stale traditions, all of them exploring new ways for the future.

The old empires in America and India had long either been lost or integrated into the European system when the Western nations began a second round of modern empire building toward the end of the nineteenth century. In a quarter century almost all of Africa was carved up and portioned out to be colonies of European nations, and in that same period Asia as well was divided into spheres of influence and trade. While the two old established Asian nations—China and Japan—remained independent, they were also deeply affected and changed by Western imperialism. China was opened to trade and to Western concessions, leading to a violent native rebellion and to a revolution that toppled the Manchu Dynasty and established a Chinese republic. Japan opened up to the modern world to the extent that it adopted Western military, educational, governmental, and financial ways, even to the extent of taking colonies of its own in China and Korea.

Amid this ferment and expansionism the clouds of war were gathering. The great nations of Europe, competing with and fearing each other, formed defensive alliances with friends against foes and stockpiled weapons for a conflict that seemed to be more inevitable by the certainty of combatants that it could not be avoided.

Identify:

1. Quanta [p. 488] *– Max Planck*
    – energy is radiated discontinuously in irregular packets of energy that he called quanta.

2. Relativity [p. 488] *Theory discovered by Albert Einstein*
    – space + time are not absolute but relative to the observer + are interwoven into a four dimensional space-time continuum.

3. Repression [pp. 489-490]

4. *Volk* [pp. 490-491] *German for nation, people or race.*
    – underlying idea in German history since beginning of the 19th

5. Naturalism [p. 490]
    – material world was accepted as real + literature was realistic to Naturalists.

6. Leo XIII [p. 491]
    Pope Leo permitted the teaching of evolution as a hypothesis in Catholic school.

7. Post-Impressionism [pp. 492-493]
    retained Impressionist emphasis on light + colour but revolutionized it even further by paying more attention to structure + form.

8. Florence Nightingale [p. 495]
    British nurse – efforts in Crimean war transformed nursing into a profession of well-trained, middle class women in white.

9. Emmeline Pankhurst [p. 495]
    – + her daughters founded the Women's Social + Political Union

10. Zionism [pp. 496-497]
    Jews to Palestine.

11. Imperialism [pp. 500-506]
    intense scramble for overseas territory Europeans to carve up Asia & Africa

12. Rhodesia [p. 502]
    Cecil Rhodes
    British policy in southern Africa – was largely determined by him.

Match the following words with their definitions:

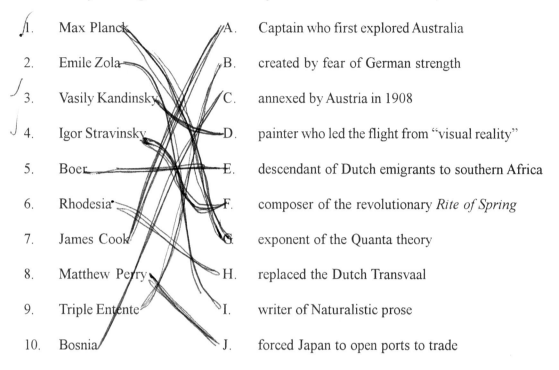

1. Max Planck
2. Emile Zola
3. Vasily Kandinsky
4. Igor Stravinsky
5. Boer
6. Rhodesia
7. James Cook
8. Matthew Perry
9. Triple Entente
10. Bosnia

A. Captain who first explored Australia

B. created by fear of German strength

C. annexed by Austria in 1908

D. painter who led the flight from "visual reality"

E. descendant of Dutch emigrants to southern Africa

F. composer of the revolutionary *Rite of Spring*

G. exponent of the Quanta theory

H. replaced the Dutch Transvaal

I. writer of Naturalistic prose

J. forced Japan to open ports to trade

Multiple-Choice:

1. Max Planck's discovery of "quanta" energy

    a. brought Newtonian physics into serious question.
    b. proved that atoms are the building blocks of matter.
    c. questioned the Darwinian theory of energy.
    d. led to massive demonstrations in Russia.

2. Albert Einstein

    a. worked with Max Planck to develop the quantum theory.
    b. was, from the beginning, welcomed into the European scientific community.
    c. developed a theory in which neither time nor space exists independent of human experience.
    d. maintained the Newtonian scheme of the universe as one with absolute time and space.

3.   Sigmund Freud believed that the way to solve the conflicts of his psychologically disturbed patients was to

    a.   trace repression back to its childhood origins.
    b.   use electrotherapy along with drugs.
    c.   help them override the pleasure principle.
    d.   separate them from their superegos.

4.   Exponents of Social Darwinism in the late nineteenth century advocated

    a.   international struggle to establish what peoples are fittest to survive.
    b.   Communist expansion as the only way to help those who are economically weak.
    c.   a moratorium on war in order to save mankind from destruction.
    d.   national medical care programs for those unable to pay for it themselves.

5.   The German concept of the *Volk*

    a.   proclaimed that German culture to be the world's most advanced.
    b.   led to the belief that the Jews were out to destroy the Aryan race.
    c.   represented the direction Social Darwinism took in that country.
    d.   all of the above

6.   Zola's literary Naturalism was deeply influenced by

    a.   Freud's theory of the unconscious.
    b.   Herzl's call for a Jewish state.
    c.   Darwin's theory of the struggle for survival.
    d.   Nietzsche's call for a superman.

7.   The early feminist movement was known for

    a.   sharing identical goals with the trade union movement.
    b.   achievements in nursing by Nightingale and Sieveking.
    c.   iconoclastic speeches by the German leader Millicent Fawcett.
    d.   achieving woman suffrage across Europe by 1914.

8.   Theodor Herzl's *Jewish State* concluded that

    a.   Jews should remain in Europe and wait for the tide of anti-Semitism to turn.
    b.   the Zionist movement was a Utopian dream that should best be abandoned.
    c.   the creation of a Jewish nation in Palestine was both feasible and advisable.
    d.   a separate Jewish homeland would never be tolerated by the European nations.

9.   Which of the following statements best applies to European imperialism in Asia?

    a.   Russia showed little interest in Asia until 1918.
    b.   The British acquired the Philippines in a war with Spain.
    (c.)   China was divided by the great powers into spheres of influence.
    d.   The United States dominated Southeast Asia after 1895.

10.   Following the dismissal of Bismarck by William II in 1890, Germany

    (a.)   became increasingly active in foreign affairs, pursuing its "place in the sun."
    b.   became ever more closely allied with Britain.
    c.   abandoned plans for building a navy and concentrated fully on building its army.
    d.   succeeded in splitting the Entente Cordiale agreed to by Britain and France.

Complete the following sentences:

1.   Max Planck concluded that bodies radiate energy in irregular packets called _atoms_ _quanta_, thus creating questions about the old view of ~~physics~~ and the theories of _Newton_.

2.   Einstein's special theory of _relativity_ said space and time are not absolute, but depend upon the _observer_; he elaborated that if matter disappeared, so too would _time_ and _space_.

3.   Freud taught that human behavior is largely affected by the _unconscious_, containing memory of experiences of that we are _oblivious_, but that often appear in coded form in our _dreams_.

4.   Friedrich von Bernhardi added to the theory of Social _Darwinism_ the claim that war is a _biological_ _necessity_, for it is creative, "the _father_ of all things."

5.   Pope Leo XIII upheld the right of private _property_, yet found fault with what he called "naked" _capitalism_. He identified as Christian many of the ideas of _Marx/Socialism_, but he condemned _Marx_ for being materialistic and anti-religious.

6.   Pissarro and the Impressionists painted nature directly, seeking to show the changing effects of _light_ on material objects. Berthe Morisot believed that women have a special _vision_, more _delicate_ than that of men.

7.   The "new imperialism" of the late nineteenth century involved European domination of
      Asia and _Africa_, two areas largely ignored by earlier
      imperialistic ventures. At this time there was a mad, competitive _race_ for
      new colonies.

8.   The Boers made their Great Trek and set up governments in the _Transvaal_ and
      the _Orange_ _Free_ _State_ in order to avoid
      British rule.

9.   Two former British colonies granted virtual independence at the turn of the century were the
      Commonwealth of _Australia_ in 1901 and the Dominion of _South African_
      New Zealand in 1907.

10.   Early in the twentieth century a crisis in the _Balkans_ threatened the peace when
      Austria decided to annex _Bosnia_ and _Herzegovina_.

Place the following in chronological order and give dates:

1.   First Zionist Congress   1.

2.   Russo-Japanese War   2.

3.   British take Hong Kong   3.

4.   Japan annexes Korea   4.

5.   Victoria crowned Empress of India   5.

6.   Suez Canal opened   6.

7.   Triple Entente formed   7.

Questions for Critical Thought: In each essay, fully explore the topic by answering the questions
that follow it.

1.   The Intellectual Ferment in Late Nineteenth Century Science. What new ideas and theories
      were introduced into the world of science at this time? How did Einstein change the study of
      physics? How did the world of science spawn the new field of psychotherapy? What did
      Freud's theories add to the study of the human species? What long-range effects did the
      discoveries and theories of Einstein and Freud have on the world of science?

2.   Racism in the Late Nineteenth Century. How did the Social Darwinists give legitimacy to a new wave of racism in Europe? What is anti-Semitism, and why were the Jews especially singled out for persecution? What response did Theodor Herzl make to this racism? What were the goals of Zionism? What were the obstacles to those goals? Why did it not disappear?

3.   Feminism at the Turn of the Century. What conditions and opportunities brought about the movement called feminism? Who were its leaders, and what were their goals? How did the movement affect women's lives at the time, and what were its long-range accomplishments?

4.   The "New Imperialism" of the Late Nineteenth Century. How did the new wave of imperialism differ from earlier imperialistic ventures? Why and how did Europeans move into Africa and Asia? What did they accomplish on those continents? How did imperialistic structures differ in various parts of the world? What were the reactions of native peoples in each place?

Analysis of Primary Source Documents:

1.   What do you learn of Freud's methodology by reading his lecture on repression? What explanation do you find here for the immense prestige he gained in his own lifetime?

2.   How would a typical woman of 1879 have felt watching Ibsen's *A Doll's House*? What might "Nora" have said to women had she turned to address the audience directly?

3.   What specifically was Kipling's "white man's burden," how were white men to bear it, and what would be their reward?

4.   In his 1908 interview with the British *Daily Telegraph*, Kaiser Wilhelm II spoke his mind. What did he mean to say, and how did he end up saying it? How do you account for the difference?

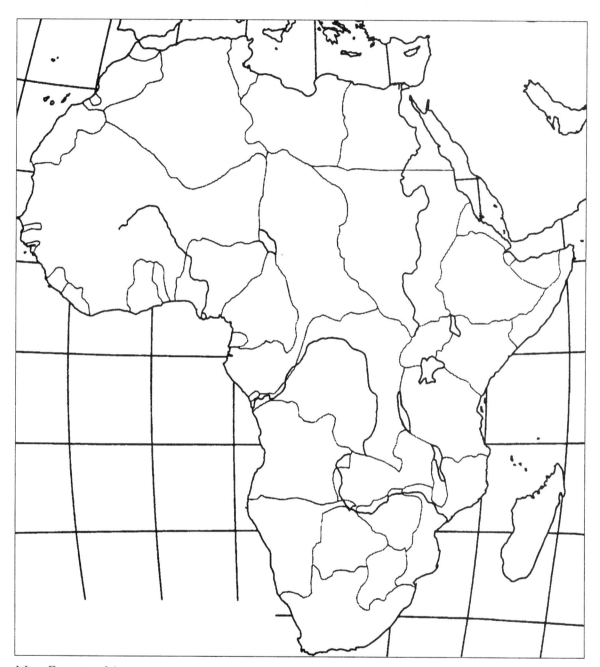

Map Exercise 14

Map Exercise 14:   Africa in 1914

Using various colors of pencil, shade the foreign possessions of each nation:

1.   Britain
2.   Belgium
3.   France
4.   Germany
5.   Italy
6.   Portugal
7.   Spain

Label the following colonies:

1.   Algeria
2.   Angola
3.   Cameroon
4.   Congo
5.   Egypt
6.   Eritrea
7.   German East Africa
8.   Guinea
9.   Kenya
10.   Libya
11.   Madagascar
12.   Morocco
13.   Mozambique
14.   Nigeria
15.   Rio de Oro
16.   Senegal
17.   Sierra Leone
18.   Somaliland
19.   South Africa
20.   South West Africa
21.   Tunis
22.   Uganda

25 THE BEGINNING OF THE TWENTIETH-CENTURY CRISIS: WAR AND REVOLUTION

Chapter Outline:

I.   The Road to World War I
    A.   Nationalism and Internal Dissent
    B.   Militarism
    C.   Outbreak of War: The Summer of 1914
        1.   Austria's Troubles in the Balkans
        2.   The Assassination of Franz-Ferdinand
        3.   The Alliances Bring General War
        4.   Germany's Schlieffen Plan

II.   The War
    A.   Illusions and Stalemate: 1914-1915
        1.   Enthusiasm and Expectations for a Brief War
        2.   The French Defensive
        3.   German Successes in the East
    B.   The Great Slaughter: 1916-1917
        1.   Trench Warfare
        2.   Hardships of the Average Soldier
    C.   The Widening of the War
        1.   The Balkans and Gallipoli
        2.   The Middle East
        3.   Entry of the United States
    D.   The Impact of Total War on the Home Front
        1.   Political Centralization and Economic Regulation
        2.   Public Order and Public Opinion
        3.   Social Impact of Total War: Labor and Women

III.   War and Revolution
    A.   The Russian Revolution
        1.   March Revolution and a Provisional Government
        2.   Lenin and the Bolshevik (October) Revolution
        3.   The Treaty of Brest-Litovsk
        4.   Civil War
    B.   The Last Year of the War: 1918
        1.   Germany's Last Gamble
        2.   Armistice: November 11
        3.   The German Republic

IV.   The Paris Peace Settlement
    A.   Wilson's Ideals: The Fourteen Points
    B.   The Treaty of Versailles
    C.   Other Peace Treaties

Chapter Summary:

The twentieth century really began not in 1900, but with the outbreak of World War I in 1914. The Great War, as it was called until a second world war broke out in 1939, ended the military alliances and styles of life left over from the century past and ushered in the new world of a truly new century.

In the summer of 1914, Archduke Francis Ferdinand of Austria-Hungary was assassinated in the Bosnian capital of Sarajevo, and within six weeks the major nations of Europe were at war with each other in accordance with their myriad treaties, many of them until that time kept secret. For over a quarter of a century the growth of nationalistic competition had combined with an equally dangerous growth in military weaponry all across the continent, and this made Europe a powder keg waiting to burst into flames. The assassination was the spark needed for ignition.

Since Germany had no trouble defeating Russian armies, it became evident quite early in the conflict that the war would be won and lost on the Western Front, between Germany and the Allies, Britain and France. Yet the war dragged on for four long years, much of it fought from trenches, as morale dropped lower and lower. Unrest spread through both camps and at home, where the belligerents had to keep their civilian populations in line with unusually harsh measures. Only in Russia did the government lose control; and there the Tsar and his family were murdered, ushering in a new regime. Out of the chaos that followed the March Revolution, Lenin's Bolshevik Party finally emerged triumphant. Russia would be a Communist state for over seventy years.

When the war eventually ended, the two losers experienced the revolutions that had threatened them during the war; and both Germany and Austria became republics. The victors met in Paris to make the peace and themselves could not agree on whether to establish a new and just world order or punish the Germans. Eventually they settled for a compromise that virtually assured there would be another world war in the near future.

Identify:

1.   Balkans   [p. 512]

2.   Black Hand   [p. 514]

3.   Schlieffen Plan   [p. 514]

4.   Gallipoli   [pp. 517-518]

5.   DORA   [p. 521]

6.   Hemophilia   [p. 523]

7.   Alexander Kerensky   [p. 523]

8.   Bolsheviks   [pp. 523-525]

9.   Lenin   [pp. 524-525]

10.   Brest-Litovsk   [pp. 525-526]

11.   Leon Trotsky   [pp. 525-526]

12.   Friedrich Ebert   [p. 527]

13.   League of Nations   [pp. 528, 531]

14.   War Guilt Clause   [p. 529]

Match the following words with their definitions:

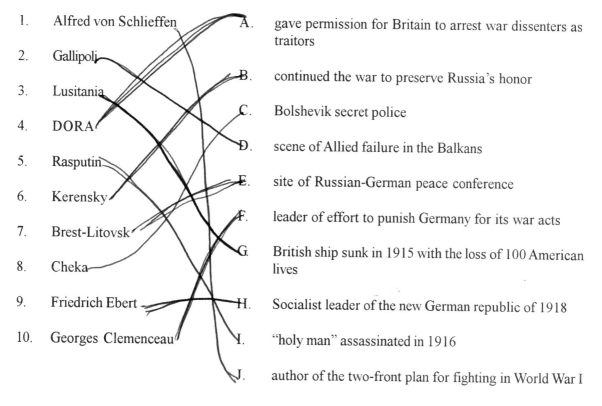

1.   Alfred von Schlieffen

2.   Gallipoli

3.   Lusitania

4.   DORA

5.   Rasputin

6.   Kerensky

7.   Brest-Litovsk

8.   Cheka

9.   Friedrich Ebert

10. Georges Clemenceau

A.   gave permission for Britain to arrest war dissenters as traitors

B.   continued the war to preserve Russia's honor

C.   Bolshevik secret police

D.   scene of Allied failure in the Balkans

E.   site of Russian-German peace conference

F.   leader of effort to punish Germany for its war acts

G.   British ship sunk in 1915 with the loss of 100 American lives

H.   Socialist leader of the new German republic of 1918

I.   "holy man" assassinated in 1916

J.   author of the two-front plan for fighting in World War I

Multiple-Choice:

1.   The historian Arnold Toynbee has said that before the outbreak of World War I in 1914, the attitude of most Europeans was

   a.   highly optimistic, expecting material progress and a "utopian" future.
   b.   extremely indifferent to things in the future.
   c.   extremely negative, believing the end of the world was probably near.
   d.   contented dependence on the good graces of socialistic governments.

2.   The immediate cause of the start of World War I was

   a.   an uprising of peasants in Catholic Bavaria.
   b.   the assassination of Archduke Francis Ferdinand.
   c.   the German invasion of Poland.
   d.   a German naval blockade of Britain.

3.   During the first year in World War I

     a.   the First Battle of the Marne left the Western Front in stalemate.
     b.   Italy switched to the German and Austrian side.
     c.   the German army took heavy losses on the Russian Front.
     d.   Serbia defeated Austria in the Balkans.

4.   The United States finally decided to enter the war because of

     a.   a surprise German invasion of Mexico.
     b.   Germany's refusal to stop unrestricted submarine warfare.
     c.   President Wilson's dream of an American Empire.
     d.   the assassination of the American ambassador in Vienna.

5.   The entry of the United States into World War I

     a.   gave the Allies a much needed psychological boost.
     b.   made the German Naval Staff suggest immediate surrender.
     c.   came in response to Turkey's entrance on the side of Germany.
     d.   put an end to Germany's use of submarine warfare.

6.   As public morale weakened in the later stages of the war

     a.   workers' strikes lessened because of brutal suppression.
     b.   Clemenceau's French government let leftists dictate government policy.
     c.   propaganda posters were widely ridiculed and discontinued.
     d.   police powers were expanded to include the arrest of dissenters as traitors.

7.   The most visible effect of the war on European society was

     a.   an end to unemployment.
     b.   an end to street crime.
     c.   a dramatic increase in church attendance.
     d.   a new positive outlook by young people.

8.   Which of the following best describes the wartime Russian government?

     a.   "Holy man" Rasputin ran the bureaucracy efficiently.
     b.   The Tsarina Alexandra kept Nicholas ignorant of domestic problems.
     c.   The general population was supportive throughout the war.
     d.   Numerous reforms kept the peasants happy.

9.   Which of the following statements best applies to Lenin?

    a.   He was a central figure in the Provisional Government.
    b.   In his "April Theses" he denounced revolutionary violence.
    c.   His middle-class background made him want to establish a democratically-elected Russian Legislature.
    d.   He promised that the Bolsheviks would redistribute all Russian lands to the peasants.

10.   At the end of the war, Woodrow Wilson wanted most of all to

    a.   punish Germany.
    b.   assure self-determination for all peoples.
    c.   strengthen America's influence in Europe.
    d.   bring down the Soviet Union.

Complete the following sentences:

1.   Among the ethnic minorities hoping in 1914 for nationhood were the ___Irish___ in Britain, the ___Poles___ in Russia, and the ___Slavs___ in Austria-Hungary.

2.   Archduke Francis Ferdinand's assassin was a ___Bosnian___ who worked for a ___Serbian___ terrorist organization called the ___Black Hand___.

3.   The German army was halted twenty miles from ___Paris___ at the ___Marne___ River and there followed a long period of ___trench___ warfare.

4.   As the war escalated, British officer T. E. ___Lawrence___ inspired Arab princes to revolt against their ___Ottoman___ overlords.

5.   The United States, upset in 1915 over the sinking of the ___Lusitania___, was at last drawn into World War I in April, 1917 by the German decision to use unrestricted ___submarine___ ___warfare___.

6.   DORA allowed British ___dissenters___ to be arrested, newspapers to be ___censored___, and at times publications to be ___suspended___.

7.   The Russian Duma in March 1917 created a ___provisional___ ___government___, which forced the Tsar to ___abdicate___.

8.   The government of Alexander Kerensky was overthrown by the _Bolshevik_ led by _Lenin_, who surrendered to Germany at _Brest-Litovsk_.

9.   American President Woodrow Wilson came to Paris with a plan for peace, his _Fourteen Points_, but he was met by resistance from leaders of _Britain_ and _France_ whose priority was to punish Germany.

10.   Clemenceau wanted to _demilitarize_ Germany and make her pay vast _reparations_ to the victors. He also, at first, demanded the creation of a separate _Rhineland_.

Place the following in chronological order and give dates:

1.   Treaty of Brest-Litovsk signed   1.

2.   Armistice between Allies and Germany   2.

3.   Battle at Gallipoli begins   3.

4.   Paris Conference begins   4.

5.   Archduke Francis Ferdinand assassinated   5.

6.   War begins between Germany and Russia   6.

7.   The United States enters the war   7.

Questions for Critical Thought: In each essay, fully explore the topic by answering the questions that follow it.

1.   The Outbreak of World War I. What social, economic, political, and military conditions made a European war likely in 1914? Why does this war seem to us (who view it through hindsight) inevitable? What immediate series of events set it off?

2.   The Great War. What countries played major roles in this war? Who were their leaders, and how did each affect the conduct of the war? What were the decisive events that determined the outcome? Why did it go on for so long, and what eventually brought it to an end?

3.   The Russian Revolution. What conditions in Russia led to its revolution? How did the war hasten the coming of revolution? Who were the main players in the drama? How do the events of those days help explain the kind of nation Russia has been through most of the twentieth century and still is today?

4.   The Paris Peace Conference. What leaders gathered at Versailles in 1919 to make the peace? What ideas did each bring to the table? What conflicts arose? What were the compromises made in order to get a treaty? What did this treaty mean for the future of Europe? Was there any way to avoid what happened at Versailles?

Analysis of Primary Source Documents:

1.   Why would you know, had you not been told, that Remarque himself had known trench warfare? Why is his account of it so powerful?

2.   What does Naomi Loughnan indicate she learned in her munitions factory about working-class men and women? What did various classes and genders learn from each other there?

3.   From John Reed's account, what do you think made Lenin the leader of the Russian Revolution? What does Reed mean by Lenin's "intellect"?

4.   How did Woodrow Wilson and Georges Clemenceau differ in their assessments of the war? Why did Clemenceau consider Wilson naïve and Wilson consider Clemenceau a vindictive bigot?

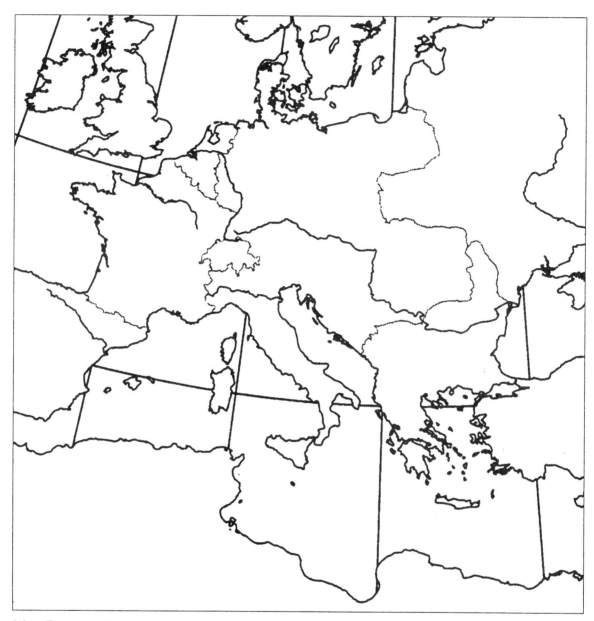

Map Exercise 15

Map Exercise 15: Europe in 1914

Using various colors of pencil, shade and label the following:

1.   Austria-Hungary
2.   Belgium
3.   Britain
4.   France
5.   Germany
6.   Greece
7.   Italy
8.   Netherlands
9.   Ottoman Empire
10. Russia
11. Spain
12. Switzerland

Pinpoint and label the following:

1.	Aisne River	15.	Marne River
2.	Amiens	16.	Masurian Lakes
3.	Antwerp	17.	Mons
4.	Argonne	18.	Moscow
5.	Berlin	19.	Nancy
6.	Brest-Litovsk	20.	Oise River
7.	Brussels	21.	Paris
8.	Calais	22.	St-Mihiel
9.	Chateau Thierry	23.	Sedan
10.	Cologne	24.	Seine River
11.	Frankfurt	25.	Somme River
12.	Gallipoli	26.	Tannenberg
13.	Le Havre	27.	Versailles
14.	Luxemburg	28.	Vienna

CHAPTER
26 THE FUTILE SEARCH FOR A NEW STABILITY: EUROPE BETWEEN THE WARS, 1919-1939

Chapter Outline:

I.   An Uncertain Peace: The Search for Security
    A.   French Policy of Coercion
        1.   Reparations and Occupation
        2.   The Locarno Treaty
    B.   The Great Depression
        1.   The Stock Market Crash
        2.   Governmental Inaction

II. The Democratic States
    A.   Great Britain and Keynesian Economics
    B.   France and the Popular Front
    C.   The United States and Roosevelt's New Deal

III. Retreat from Democracy: Authoritarian and Totalitarian States
    A.   Fascist Italy
        1.   The Anger of Post-war Italy
        2.   Benito Mussolini and the Italian Fascist State
        3.   Fascism and Women
        4.   Fascism and the Catholic Church
    B.   Hitler and Nazi Germany
        1.   The Weimar Republic and the Rise of the Nazis
        2.   National Socialism
            a.   Anti-communism and the Reichstag Fire
            b.   Enabling Act and Totalitarian Rule
        3.   The Nazi State, 1933-1939
            a.   Hitler Youth and League of German Maidens
            b.   Anti-Semitism and *Kristallnacht*

C.   Soviet Russia
1.   Lenin's New Economic Policy
2.   The Stalin Era
D.   Authoritarian States

IV. The Expansion of Mass Culture and Mass Leisure
A.   Radio and Movies
B.   Mass Leisure: *Kraft durch Freude*

V. Cultural and Intellectual Trends in the Interwar Years
A.   Nightmares and New Visions: Art and Music
1.   Dadaism and Surrealism in Art
2.   Functionalism in Architecture
3.   Socialist Realism
4.   Schönberg and Atonal Music
5.   The Search for the Unconscious
B.   Jungian Psychology
C.   The Heroic Age of Physics
1.   Ernest Rutherford and the Atom
2.   Werner Heisenberg's Uncertainty Principle

Chapter Summary:

Most intelligent observers knew by 1919 that the treaty that ended World War I was flawed. The French, who felt vulnerable to another invasion and abandoned by their former allies, sought to weaken Germany and punish her for past offenses, leading to hostilities on both sides. There were a few hopeful years, during the late 1920s, when material prosperity seemed to return, but then the Great Depression following the stock market crash of 1929 brought Europe back to the brink of ruin—economic, social, and political.

The democracies—Britain, France, the Scandinavian countries, and the United States—spent most of the 1930s trying to recover from the crash of 1929, while eastern and southern European nations turned ever more to authoritarian and totalitarian governments. Following the lead of Fascist Italy, Germany surrendered to Nazi rule. Communism in Russia took a turn to the right under Stalin's iron fist. While Fascism and Communism espoused widely different philosophies of economics and government, they showed striking similarities in their treatment of their people. Democracy seemed to be on the wane.

Popular culture reflected the deepening pessimism of the 1930s. While entertainment was accessible to more people than ever before through rapid increases in the numbers of movie theaters and radios, and there was more time and opportunity for leisure activities than ever, people still seemed driven to the pursuit of happiness as if it might all soon end. Film, radio, and leisure were used by the totalitarian regimes to increase their power. The arts, literature, and music reflected the pessimism and irrationality of the day; physics continued to develop methods that might just as well destroy as save the world. Thunderclouds gathered.

Identify:

1.   Gustav Stresemann   [p. 534]

2.   Aristide Briand   [p. 535]

3.   Popular Front   [pp. 536-537]

4.   New Deal   [p. 538]

5.   Benito Mussolini   [pp. 538-540]

6.   Fascism   [pp. 538-540]

7.   Weimar Republic   [pp. 540-541]

8.   Beer Hall *Putsch*   [p. 541]

9.   *Mein Kampf*   [p. 541]

10.   *Gleichschaltung*   [p. 542]

11.   *Kristallnacht*   [p. 545]

12.   NEP   [p. 545]

13.   Francisco Franco   [p. 548]

14.   Surrealism   [p. 550]

Match the following words with their definitions:

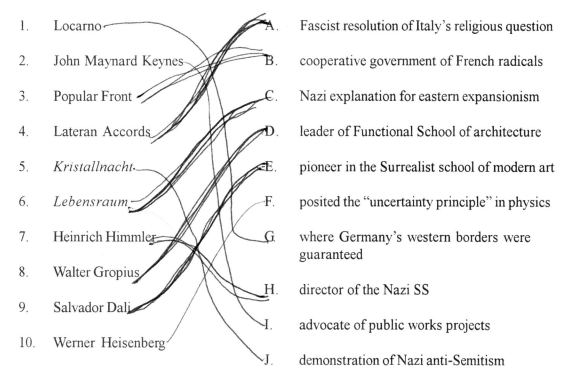

1.	Locarno	A.	Fascist resolution of Italy's religious question
2.	John Maynard Keynes	B.	cooperative government of French radicals
3.	Popular Front	C.	Nazi explanation for eastern expansionism
4.	Lateran Accords	D.	leader of Functional School of architecture
5.	*Kristallnacht*	E.	pioneer in the Surrealist school of modern art
6.	*Lebensraum*	F.	posited the "uncertainty principle" in physics
7.	Heinrich Himmler	G.	where Germany's western borders were guaranteed
8.	Walter Gropius		
9.	Salvador Dali	H.	director of the Nazi SS
10.	Werner Heisenberg	I.	advocate of public works projects
		J.	demonstration of Nazi anti-Semitism

Multiple-Choice:

1. Efforts to maintain peace following World War I included:

    a. a three-power alliance of Britain, France, and Germany.
    b. the development of a peace-keeping League of Nations Army.
    c. French efforts to keep Germany weak.
    d. continued involvement of the United States in European affairs.

2. A major cause of the Great Depression was

    a. European unconcern for Asian affairs.
    b. the recall of American loans from European markets.
    c. high prices of agricultural products from eastern Europe.
    d. the Keynesian philosophy of free markets.

3.   Economist John Maynard Keynes suggested that a way out of the Great Depression might be a

    a.   system of planned unemployment.
    b.   program of strict austerity to toughen the economy.
    c.   government program of public works.
    d.   series of government loans to business.

4.   One overall effect of the Great Depression in Europe was

    a.   the fall of all Communist governments.
    b.   high unemployment everywhere except in Britain.
    c.   a strengthening of liberal democracies.
    d.   the rise of fascist movements and governments.

5.   Which of the following statements best describes Mussolini's Italian Fascist state?

    a.   Government control of the mass media allowed the state successfully to integrate the masses into its programs.
    b.   Fascist propaganda, laws, and practices attempted to force women out of factories and to stay at home.
    c.   Giuseppe Bottai's radical education policies enabled the state to create thousands of "new Fascist men."
    d.   All religion, including Catholicism, was seen as the enemy of the state.

6.   The Lateran Accords of 1929

    a.   nationalized all church property.
    b.   recognized Catholicism as the sole religion of Italy.
    c.   coincided with the Catholic Church's official condemnation of Fascism.
    d.   eliminated all government support for the Catholic Church.

7.   Heinrich Himmler was responsible for

    a.   forming Nazi professional organizations to serve the state.
    b.   carrying out SS operations of social and racial terror.
    c.   chairing the German Labor Front.
    d.   organizing the Hitler Youth organization.

8. Stalin made his way to power in the Soviet Union as

   a. Secretary of the Communist Party.
   b. Commissioner of Labor, building the Moscow subway.
   c. Defense Minister, successfully defeating the Poles.
   d. Director of the Corps of Engineers, building dams.

9. The Spanish Civil War ended with the victory of

   a. King Alfonso XIII and General Primo de Rivera.
   b. an antifascist coalition, aided by Soviet troops.
   c. the national front, aided by Italy and Germany.
   d. General Francisco Franco, who established an authoritarian regime.

10. *Kraft durch Freude* was a program designed by the Nazi government to

    a. increase the number of children each family produced.
    b. increase military awareness and preparedness.
    c. expand production in factories.
    d. provide civilian recreation and to mold public opinion.

Complete the following sentences:

1. Although Woodrow Wilson originated the idea of a __league__ of __Nations__, his country's failure to join it and refusal to honor defensive military alliances left __France__ insecure and bitter, determined to keep __Germany__ weak.

2. When Germany could not pay further __reparations__, France occupied the __Ruhr__ Valley, and Germany then fueled __inflation__ by printing more paper money.

3. John Maynard Keynes argued that unemployment stemmed from decline in __demand__, and that this could be remedied by __public works__ projects, which could be financed by __deficit spending__.

4. The French Popular Front introduced new benefit programs for the __working__ class, sometimes called the French __New Deal__.

5. After Mussolini was expelled from the ___Socialist___ Party, he founded his
    ___Fascist___ Party, whose followers called him ___Il   Duce___.

6. In order to create his perfect Aryan state, the Nazis built death camps for ___Jews___,
    controlled citizens with secret police directed by ___Heinrich   Himmler___,
    and trained children for Nazi service in the ___Hitler   Youth___.

7. By 1929 Stalin had secured power in Russia by eliminating all Old ___Bolsheviks___ from
    power, particularly his chief rival ___Leon   Trotsky___, and launched a
    series of plans to ___industrialize___ Russia and ___collectivize___ farming.

8. Totalitarian regimes used recreation to mold their populations into willing servants of the state,
    as is seen in the Nazi program ___Kraft   Durch   Freude___.

9. The rebellious art movement called Dadaism tried to show the ___purposlessness___ of life:
    Surrealism tried to visualize the ___unconscious___; and the Bauhaus architects stripped
    away all ___ornamentation___ in order to follow pure function.

10. In his masterpiece ___Ulysses___, the Irish exile James Joyce demonstrated the use of
    a literary "stream of ___consciousness___" that would become a part of modern literature,
    using characters from his native city ___Dublin___.

Place the following in chronological order and give dates:

1. *Kristallnacht* in Germany   1.

2. Hitler becomes ruler of Germany   2.

3. Fascist dictatorship established in Italy   3.

4. National Government coalition begins in Britain   4.

5. Popular Front formed in France   5.

6. Franklin Roosevelt elected president   6.
    of the United States

7. Death of Lenin   7.

Questions for Critical Thought: In each essay, fully explore the topic by answering the questions that follow it.

1.   The Great Depression. What caused the financial collapse of 1929? How did the democracies react to the crisis, and how did their reactions change them? What were the reactions to it in southern and central Europe? In what ways did the Depression lead to World War II?

2.   Fascism. What were the conditions that led to the successes of European Fascism? Who were its major spokesmen and leaders? What were their goals? What were the consequences of Fascist takeovers in Italy and Germany to those countries, to the democracies, to minorities, and eventually to the United States?

3.   Stalinist Russia. How did Stalin come to power in the Soviet Union? What were his goals and programs? Why did his regime have appeal in the West during the Depression? What were the consequences of his presence in the modern world?

4.   New Visions in the Arts. What were the assumptions and philosophies behind Dadaism, Surrealism, the Bauhaus School, and the writings of James Joyce and Hermann Hesse? What ideas from outside the arts influenced them? What historical events influenced them? How did they reflect their world in their time? How did they influence it?

Analysis of Primary Source Documents:

1.   What were the effects of unemployment during the Great Depression? How would a fascist politician have appealed for the votes of unemployed men?

2.   What, according to Hitler, did mass political meetings accomplish? How did Hitler tailor his speeches to make maximum use of them?

3.   Explain the purpose of Soviet collective farms, how they worked, and why there was continual peasant resistance to them.

4.   Why did the writings of Hermann Hesse attract so many young readers? Why do they continue to do so today?

27 THE DEEPENING OF THE EUROPEAN CRISIS: WORLD WAR II

Chapter Outline:

III.   The Nazi New Order
    A.   The Nazi Empire
        1.   Conquest of "Inferior" Peoples
        2.   The Use of Foreign Labor
    B.   The Holocaust
        1.   Aryan Supremacy
        2.   Emigration: The Madagascar Plan
        3.   The Final Solution
        4.   Concentration Camps: Experimentation and Death

IV.   The Home Front
    A.   The Mobilization of Peoples
        1.   Supercentralization in the Soviet Empire
        2.   Mobilization of the American Economy
        3.   Total Mobilization in Germany
    B.   The Frontline Civilians: The Bombing of Cities
        1.   Attack Upon London
        2.   British Retaliation Against German Cities
        3.   The Bombing of Japan and the Atomic Attack Upon Hiroshima and Nagasaki

V.   The Aftermath of the War: The Emergence of the Cold War
    A.   The Conferences at Teheran, Yalta, and Potsdam
    B.   The "Iron Curtain"

Chapter Summary:

World War II was the eruption of long simmering animosities and frustrations; its outcome, both decisive and ambiguous, determined the course of European history for the next fifty years. It was also, in a real sense, the only truly world war in human history, and it helped set the global agenda for the rest of the twentieth century.

If we were to name one person as the key to the war, it would be Germany's Adolf Hitler. Germany's bitterness over the outcome of the first war would indeed have been present without Hitler, as would Germany's industrial might and capacity to wage war, as would the vacuum of power in central Europe. However, Hitler and his Nazi Party gave voice and direction to these potentially dangerous factors. Understanding how reluctant the democracies were to fight another war, he moved to enlarge the frontiers of his Third Reich until his aggression was no longer tolerable and war began.

The first two years of the war, following the invasion of Poland in September of 1939, belonged to the Axis nations—Germany, Italy, and Japan. All the victories were theirs. Not until early in 1942, with America now allied to Britain and the Soviet Union, did the war turn. After Hitler's failure in Russia, after Italy's failure to resist Allied forces in North Africa, after the United

States gained sea superiority against Japan, and after the Allies successfully invaded France, the war wound down to its conclusion.

The Nazi Empire had done its bloody worst in all the lands it had held. Despite the effectiveness of resistance movements everywhere, Nazi forces dominated much of the continent for five years, bringing oppression and death to Jews, minorities, and all "inferior" peoples. Indiscriminate bombing of civilian areas by both sides led to a tragic number of innocent deaths. World War II was costly in every way.

Even before the German and Japanese surrender, the victors were having trouble agreeing on the post-war world; and at the various conferences held to determine borders and governments it was evident that a separation between East and West was inevitable. World War II was ending as tragically as World War I. The Cold War was beginning.

Identify:

1.   Anti-Comintern Pact   [pp. 556-557]

2.   Neville Chamberlain   [p. 558]

3.   Sudetenland   [p. 558]

4.   *Blitzkrieg*   [p. 560]

5.   Henri Pétain   [p. 560]

6.   *Luftwaffe*   [p. 560]

7.   Pearl Harbor   [p. 561]

8.   El Alamein   [p. 563]

9.   Midway   [p. 563]

10.   Stalingrad   [pp. 563,565]

11.   Holocaust   [pp. 567-570]

12.   Night Witches   [p. 570]

13.   Dresden   [pp. 572-573]

14.   Hiroshima   [p. 573]

Match the following words with their definitions:

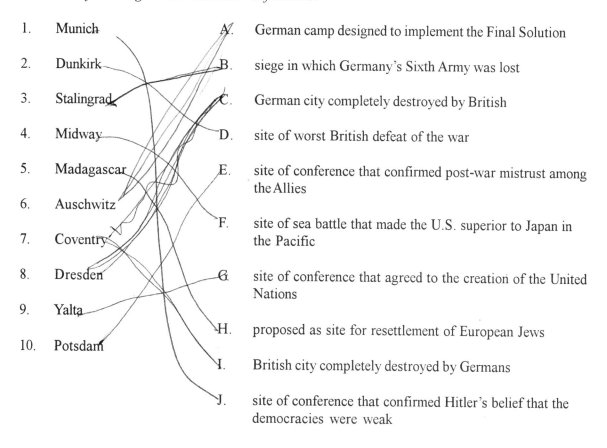

1.   Munich

2.   Dunkirk

3.   Stalingrad

4.   Midway

5.   Madagascar

6.   Auschwitz

7.   Coventry

8.   Dresden

9.   Yalta

10.   Potsdam

A.   German camp designed to implement the Final Solution

B.   siege in which Germany's Sixth Army was lost

C.   German city completely destroyed by British

D.   site of worst British defeat of the war

E.   site of conference that confirmed post-war mistrust among the Allies

F.   site of sea battle that made the U.S. superior to Japan in the Pacific

G.   site of conference that agreed to the creation of the United Nations

H.   proposed as site for resettlement of European Jews

I.   British city completely destroyed by Germans

J.   site of conference that confirmed Hitler's belief that the democracies were weak

Multiple-Choice:

1.   When Hitler came to power, Germany was

    a.   the most powerful state in Europe.
    b.   limited by the Treaty of Versailles to an army of 100,000.
    c.   threatened by Poland and Czechoslovakia.
    d.   already massing troops in the Rhineland.

2.   The Munich Conference was

    a.   applauded by Churchill as a "wise and noble experiment."
    b.   successful in keeping the Germans out of the Sudetenland.
    c.   criticized by Churchill for setting a bad precedent.
    d.   a severe political setback for Hitler at home.

3.   Following the Allied evacuation at Dunkirk, France

    a.   soon surrendered and the Vichy government was established as a puppet to Germany.
    b.   went on the offensive and stopped Germany in Normandy.
    c.   called on Italy to help them fight the Germans.
    d.   called on the Americans to move across from North Africa.

4.   The turning point of the North African campaign came

    a.   at El Alamein, where the British stopped Rommel in the summer of 1942.
    b.   when South African troops crossed the Sahara and overwhelmed Rommel.
    c.   when the free French revolted against the Vichy regime in Algeria.
    d.   when the Italians changed sides and joined the Allies in the fall of 1942.

5.   The turning point in the war for eastern Europe was the

    a.   German fiasco at Stalingrad.
    b.   German victory at Leningrad.
    c.   Russian victory at Kiev.
    d.   Russian fiasco outside Moscow.

6.   American naval superiority in the Pacific was

    a.   never in question, even after Pearl Harbor.
    b.   precarious throughout and not achieved until the very end.
    c.   achieved beyond dispute after the Battle of Midway.
    d.   not in question because the Americans had no intentions of fighting a naval war.

7.   The Nazi rule was most ruthless in

    a.   eastern Europe where the Slavs were considered racial inferiors.
    b.   France because of the age-old rivalry between the Germans and the French.
    c.   Norway, Denmark, and the Netherlands because they were so geographically near the Fatherland.
    d.   Italy because the Germans did not trust them.

8.   Nazi atrocities at Auschwitz

    a.   were largely exaggerations of war propagandists.
    b.   were willingly carried out by SS men who had few qualms about killing.
    c.   were limited to Jews, with other despised groups sent to work camps.
    (d.)   included cruel and painful "medical" experiments on inmates.

9.   Civilian bombing was carried out mainly to

    a.   reduce the number of people available to be drafted.
    b.   exact revenge on the enemy.
    (c.)   break the will of the people to resist.
    d.   satisfy the appetite of bloody leader for high death counts.

10.   The official reason for dropping atomic bombs on Japan was

    a.   to punish Japan for the bombing of Pearl Harbor.
    b.   the testing of new weapons for later battles.
    c.   the shortage of explosive materials in the U.S. arsenal.
    (d.)   to save the American lives an invasion of Japan would incur.

Complete the following sentences:

1.   In 1936 Hitler's army occupied the __Rhineland__, in 1938 he annexed
    __Austria__, and he looked next toward __Czechoslovakia__

2.   At Munich, Chamberlain followed a policy of __appeasement__ toward Hitler, boasting
    that he had achieved " __peace__ in our __times__ ."

3.   After the Nazi invasion of __Poland__ led to World War II, Hitler used "lightning
    war," or in German __Blitzkrieg__, to take Denmark, Norway, Netherlands, Belgium,
    and finally even __France__.

4.   Germany occupied three-fifths of France, but permitted the French hero of World War I,
    Henri __Petain__, to establish a government in the rest, with a capital at
    __Vichy__.

5.   War between Japan and the U.S. started with Japan's bombing of __Pearl__
    __Harbor__. Shortly thereafter Tokyo declared East Asia a __Co__ –
    __Prosperity__ __sphere__.

6. In 1942 the Allies stopped Rommel in _Nort_ _Afrie_, the German army failed to take the Russian city of _Stalingrad_, and the U.S. defeated Japan in the Battle of the _Coral_ _Sea_.

7. U.S. President Harry Truman, warned by advisers not to attempt an _invasion_ of Japan, dropped atomic bombs on _Hiroshima_ and _Nagasaki_.

8. While early suggestions such as the _Madagascar_ Plan would have sent European Jews into exile, the Final Solution as carried out by SS head _Heinrich_ _Heinrich_ was systematic _annihilation_.

9. The only World War II country to use women in combat, _Russia_, trained female pilots, called _Night_ _Witches_.

10. At Yalta, Stalin wanted post-war _spheres_ of _influence_, while Roosevelt wanted each liberated nation to have _self_ _determination_.

Place the following in chronological order and give dates:

1. German surrender at Stalingrad   1.

2. U.S. drops atomic bomb on Hiroshima   2.

3. Battle of Britain   3.

4. German occupation of the Rhineland   4.

5. Allied invasion of France   5.

6. German invasion of Poland   6.

7. Japanese attack Pearl Harbor   7.

Questions for Critical Thought: In each essay, fully explore the topic by answering the questions that follow it.

1. Steps Leading to World War II. What mistakes did the democracies make in dealing with Hitler? What were Hitler's goals, and how did he begin carrying them out? How did decisions made at Munich step up the march to war? What was the significance of the invasion of Poland in triggering the conflict?

2.   Turning Points of the War. What events led to Allied victory in North Africa? How did Hitler lose the war in the East? How did the United States gain superiority in the Pacific? What events led to the German surrender?

3.   The Nazi Empire. How was this empire built? How was it organized? What ideas shaped it? How did these ideas eventually bring its downfall? How does the Holocaust fit into the whole picture of the Nazi Empire?

4.   War Conferences. Where, and under what conditions, did the allies meet during the war and just after the war ended? What were the purposes of these conferences, what did they accomplish, and what did they fail to achieve? What crucial mistakes were made at them? What role did they play in the coming of the Cold War?

Analysis of Primary Source Documents:

1.   Compare and contrast Churchill's and Chamberlain's interpretations of the Munich agreement. Which probably sounded more plausible at the time? Why?

2.   Using the German soldier's diary, recount how and why the German army in Russia lost heart. Why do you not find this man cursing *Der Fuhrer*?

3.   Recount the systematic way people at German extermination camps were dispatched. What reasoning stood behind such a system?

4.   How did aerial bombing change the nature and character of war? Describe its effects on people in cities under bombardment.

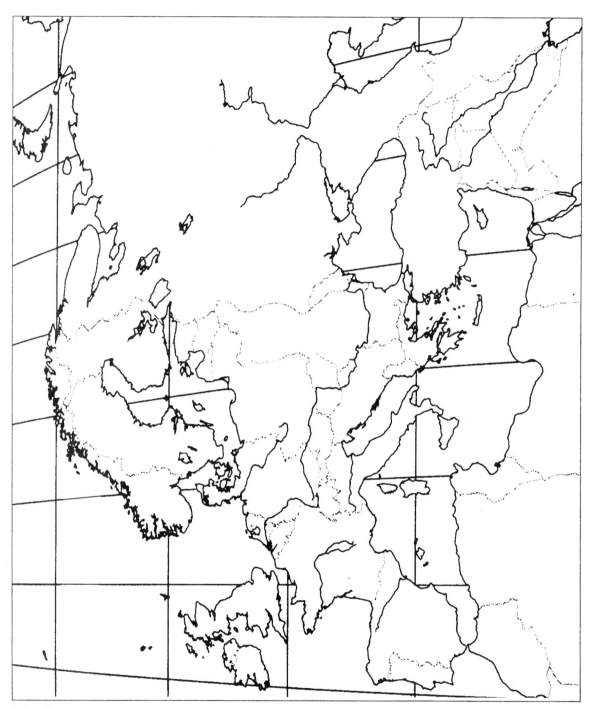

Map Exercise 16

Map Exercise 16:   World War II in Europe and North Africa

Using various colors of pencil, shade and label the following:

1.   Allied powers Britain, Portugal, the U.S.S.R., the Middle East, and areas under allied control
2.   Axis powers—Germany and Italy
3.   Axis satellites and allies
4.   Conquests made by Axis 1939-1942
5.   Neutral nations

Pinpoint and label the following:

1.   Algiers
2.   Berlin
3.   Casablanca
4.   London
5.   Moscow
6.   Paris
7.   Rome
8.   Stalingrad
9.   Tunis
10.   Warsaw

CHAPTER

28 COLD WAR AND A NEW EUROPE, 1945-1970

Chapter Outline:

I.   The Development of the Cold War
    A.   Confrontation of the Superpowers
        1.   Differing Historical Perspectives
        2.   Disagreement over Eastern Europe
        3.   Greece, Turkey, and the Truman Doctrine
        4.   Western Europe and the Marshall Plan
        5.   The Kennan Theory of Containment
        6.   The Troubled City of Berlin and the Airlift
        7.   The Creation of NATO and the Warsaw Pact
        8.   Asian Conflicts: The Korean War
        9.   Competition in Space
    B.   The Cuban Missile Crisis and Détente
        1.   Fidel Castro's Cuba
        2.   Kennedy, Khrushchev, and Crisis
        3.   U.S. Involvement in Vietnam
        4.   Steps Toward Better Relations between the Superpowers

II.   Recovery and Renewal in Europe
    A.   The End of European Colonies
        1.   Asia
        2.   Africa
        3.   "The Third World"
    B.   The Soviet Union: From Stalin to Khrushchev
        1.   Spectacular Economic Recovery
        2.   Military Buildup and Technological Advance
        3.   Khrushchev and Liberalization

4.   Eastern Europe: Behind the Iron Curtain
    a.   Tito and Yugoslavia
    b.   Stalinized States
    c.   Revolt in Czechoslovakia: "The Prague Spring"
C.   Western Europe's Revival of Democracy and the Economy
    1.   France and Charles de Gaulle
        a.   The Algerian Crisis and the Fall of the Fourth Republic
        b.   De Gaulle and the Fifth Republic
    2.   West Germany
        a.   Konrad Adenauer and the "Economic Miracle"
        b.   Denazification
    3.   Great Britain and the Welfare State
D.   Western Europe's Move Toward Unity
    1.   Experiments in Cooperation
    2.   The Common Market
E.   The United States and Canada: A New Era
    1.   American Politics and Society in the 1950s
    2.   An Age of Upheaval: America from 1960 to 1970
    3.   The Development of Canada

III.   The Emergence of a New Society
A.   The Structure of European Society
    1.   Further Urbanization
    2.   Rising Incomes and More Leisure Time
B.   New (and old) Patterns: Women in the Postwar Western World
C.   The Permissive Society
    1.   Sexual Freedom
    2.   Divorce
    3.   Drugs
D.   Education and Student Revolt

Chapter Summary:

No sooner had the Allies defeated the Central Powers than they began bickering among themselves. The democracies helped to see a Europe of representative governments and free markets, while the Soviets wanted to create a buffer against further threats from the West. In the end, what Winston Churchill called an Iron Curtain descended across the continent, separating East from West. The Cold War began.

Distrust grew as each side came to see the other as a menace to safety in the world. The Cold War, made all the more dangerous by the presence on both sides of nuclear weapons, continued through much of the rest of the twentieth century, dominating foreign policy in all

European countries. Only after the Cuban Missile Crisis of 1963, when world survival hung in the balance, did the two sides begin the first tentative steps toward détente.

Meanwhile the face of Europe was changed in the years just after the war. While the Soviet Union created Stalinist satellites out of the formerly independent nations surrounding it, the Western democracies experimented with social reform that led in many countries to the welfare state. Britain led the way by efforts, under the Labour government that came to power in the first postwar election, to provide social security for all its citizens: insurance, healthcare, pensions. Western Europe grouped together militarily in the North Atlantic Treaty Organization and economically in the organization of the Common Market.

Society changed during the period from 1945 to 1970. Citizen protests of the status quo occurred on both sides of the Iron Curtain. In Hungary and in Czechoslovakia of the Soviet bloc, in France and the United States of the West, people protesting materialism and injustice made their voices heard in demonstrations. Everywhere in the West there was more freedom, yet there was also a feeling that society had lost its way. People everywhere seemed to be looking for new solutions to an aging set of problems.

Identify:

1.   Truman Doctrine [pp. 579-580]

2.   George Kennan [pp. 580-581]

3.   Berlin air lift [p. 581]

4.   NATO [p. 582]

5.   Warsaw Pact [p. 582]

6.   *Sputnik* [p. 583]

7.   Nikita Khrushchev [pp. 583-584, 589]

8.   Alexander Dubcek [pp. 590-591]

9.   Charles de Gaulle [pp. 591-592]

10. Fifth Republic [p. 592]

11.   Konrad Adenauer   [pp. 592-593]

12.   Clement Atlee   [p. 593]

13.   EURATOM   [p. 594]

14.   Common Market   [p. 594]

Match the following words with their definitions:

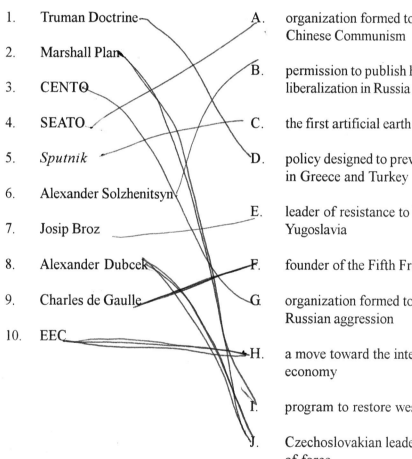

1.   Truman Doctrine

2.   Marshall Plan

3.   CENTO

4.   SEATO

5.   *Sputnik*

6.   Alexander Solzhenitsyn

7.   Josip Broz

8.   Alexander Dubcek

9.   Charles de Gaulle

10. EEC

A.   organization formed to save Asian countries from Chinese Communism

B.   permission to publish his novel demonstrated some liberalization in Russia

C.   the first artificial earth satellite

D.   policy designed to prevent Communist aggression in Greece and Turkey

E.   leader of resistance to Nazis who later ruled Yugoslavia

F.   founder of the Fifth French Republic

G.   organization formed to save the Middle East from Russian aggression

H.   a move toward the integration of the European economy

I.   program to restore western Europe's economy

J.   Czechoslovakian leader removed by Soviet show of force

Multiple-Choice:

1.   The Truman Doctrine, which promised aid to countries resisting Communist domination, came in response to threats to

      a.   Greece and Turkey.
      b.   Austria and Italy.
      c.   Lebanon and Israel.
      d.   Egypt and Iran.

2.   The Cold War struggle over Germany resulted in

      a.   the creation of an independent united Germany under Walter Ulbricht.
      b.   an East German economic miracle brought about with Soviet technological advances.
      c.   a successful blockade of West Berlin by Soviet forces.
      d.   the creation of two separate German states.

3.   One overall effect of the Korean War was

      a.   the domination of Southeast Asia by the Soviet Union.
      b.   an end to American and Soviet involvement in Asian affairs.
      c.   the reinforcement of American determination to contain Soviet power in the world.
      d.   an end to all Communist efforts to gain a foothold on the Asian continent.

4.   The United States played a dominant role in all of the following alliances *except*

      a.   NATO.
      b.   COMECON.
      c.   CENTO.
      d.   SEATO.

5.   In 1963 President Kennedy responded to proof that there were nuclear weapons in Cuba with

      a.   an order to keep it secret so as not to disturb the American public.
      b.   an invasion order that failed at the Bay of Pigs.
      c.   a blockade of the island that required Soviet ships to turn back.
      d.   an air attack that knocked out the missiles.

6.   Post-World War II life in the U.S.S.R. under Stalin saw

   a.   continued low standards of living for the working classes.
   b.   an emphasis on the production of luxury goods for domestic markets.
   c.   relaxation of restrictions on artists and writers.
   d.   the adaptation of Communism to new western European ways.

7.   The 1956 independence movement in Hungary resulted in

   a.   the end of Communist rule there.
   b.   an end to American control of the economy.
   c.   armed Soviet intervention and the reassertion of strong Communist leadership.
   d.   a revival of the Catholic faith among the Hungarian people.

8.   The 1968 Czechoslovakian "Prague Spring"

   a.   was triggered by the reforms of Alexander Dubcek.
   b.   led to the presidency in 1970 of Václav Havel.
   c.   saw Czechoslovakia withdraw from the Soviet bloc.
   d.   brought about the resignation of Gustav Husák.

9.   As President of France, Charles de Gaulle's policy toward the Cold War was to

   a.   align France with the Warsaw Pact nations.
   b.   remain independent of the superpowers.
   c.   follow the American lead throughout.
   d.   make France the leading member of NATO.

10.   Which of the following statements on postwar Britain is *false*?

   a.   National insurance and national health acts helped make Britain a welfare state.
   b.   The Conservative Party in the 1950s revoked nearly all of the socialist legislation of the Labour Party of the 1940s.
   c.   Neither Labour nor the Conservatives could solve the problems of labor, the economy, or Northern Ireland.
   d.   Churchill served a second term before retiring.

Complete the following sentences:

1. U.S. President Truman was so alarmed in 1947 by _____ inability to defend the eastern Mediterranean that he offered American aid to protect _____ and _____ against Soviet expansion.

2. U.S. diplomat George Kennan, an expert in _____ affairs, influenced American policy for decades with his article in the publication _____ _____ calling for the _____ of Communism.

3. President Kennedy's response to discovering Soviet _____ in Cuba in 1962 was to _____ the island and then agree not to _____ it.

4. Post-war decolonization of Asia saw the United States leave the _____, Britain leave _____, and France reluctantly leave _____.

5. For convenience after 1950 the industrialized nations came to be called the _____ _____, the Soviet sphere the _____ _____, and the poorer regions the _____ _____.

6. Khrushchev's era saw such a spirit of rebellion in Soviet _____ _____ that he had to crush a 1956 uprising in _____ and one in 1968 in _____.

7. To make the case that France was in the 1950s still a great power, Charles de Gaulle withdrew from _____, built _____ weapons, and increased the production and export of _____ and _____.

8. In Germany, Ludwig Erhard's work as Minister of Finance helped bring about the post-war "_____ _____," and he was rewarded by being chosen to succeed _____ _____ as chancellor.

9. The British welfare system, which inspired other European nations, nationalized the _____ of England, enacted a National _____ Act, and established a National _____ Service.

10. Across Europe various countries followed the Swedish "sexual revolution" of the 1960s by decriminalizing _____, providing more sex _____, and introducing a pill for _____ _____.

Place the following in chronological order and give dates:

1. Cuban missile crisis   1.

2. Formation of the Warsaw Pact   2.

3. Erection of the Berlin Wall   3.

4. Formation of NATO   4.

5. The Prague Spring   5.

6. Truman Doctrine outlined   6.

7. De Gaulle assumes power in France   7.

Questions for Critical Thought: In each essay, fully explore the topic by answering the questions that follow it.

1. The Origins of the Cold War. What caused the conflict between East and West called the Cold War? What divisions and contests characterized it from the late 1940s through the 1950s? Who were the major leaders on both sides, and what did they do to make things better or worse? How did this early period foreshadow the darkening picture in the 1960s and beyond?

2. The Cold War Intensified. Why did the Cold War go on for so long? Why did it never result in World War III? Who were the major leaders on both sides during the 1960s and 1970s, and what did each contribute to the conflict? What exploratory steps were taken to ease the tensions? How successful were they?

3. Social Democracy. What were the motivations for the welfare programs adopted by most Western democracies after World War II? What problems did these programs address? How successful were they? What problems did they encounter? How were ordinary citizens affected by these programs?

4. The "Permissive Society" of Post-war Europe. Why did European society change so rapidly and so completely after the war? What roots did those changes have in pre-war society? How did they affect gender roles, marriage, recreation, and student behavior?

Analysis of Primary Source Documents:

1.   Explain the Truman Doctrine. What threat provoked it, what was its intent, and where did it lead? What similar threats later appeared, and how did subsequent presidents respond to them?

2.   Compare Khrushchev's account of the Cuban Missile Crisis with what you know of the American version of this event. Who was really the aggressor, and who really won?

3.   How does the 1956 uprising against Soviet rule in Hungary look today, when Hungary seems free of foreign domination? What now appears to have been its significance?

4.   If Bob Dylan's song is an anthem for the protest movement of the 1960s, which groups did the protestors want to hear their protests, and why?

29 THE CONTEMPORARY WESTERN WORLD (SINCE 1970)

Chapter Outline:

I.   From Cold War to Post-Cold War: Toward a New World Order?
    A.   Gorbachev's "New Thinking"
    B.   The Persian Gulf War Test

II.   Toward a New European Order
    A.   Revolution in the Soviet Union
        1.   Mikhail Gorbachev: *Perestroika* and *Glasnost*
        2.   Economic Crises and Nationalist Movements
        3.   The End of the U.S.S.R.: Russia under Boris Yeltsin and Vladimir Putin
    B.   Collapse of the Communist Order in Eastern Europe
        1.   Lech Walesa's Solidarity in Poland
        2.   Václav Havel in Czechoslovakia
    C.   The Reunification of Germany
        1.   Communist Disarray
        2.   Fall of the Berlin Wall
    D.   The Disintegration of Yugoslavia
        1.   Serbian Nationalism: "Ethnic Cleansing"
        2.   War in Bosnia
        3.   War in Kosovo
    E.   Western Europe: The Winds of Change
        1.   From West Germany to Germany
        2.   Great Britain: Thatcherism
        3.   Uncertainties in France
    F.   The United States
    G.   The Development of Canada

III.   New Directions and New Problems in Western Society
    A.   Transformation in Women's Lives
    B.   The Growth of Terrorism
    C.   The Environment and the Green Movements

IV.   The World of Western Culture
    A.   Recent Trends in Art and Literature
        1.   Jackson Pollock's Abstract Impressionism
        2.   Andy Warhol's Pop Art
        3.   Samuel Becket's Theater of the Absurd
        4.   The Existentialism of Sartre and Camus
    B.   Revival of Religion
    C.   Science and Technology
        1.   The Computer
        2.   The "Small is Beautiful" Movement
    D.   Explosion of Popular Culture: The Americanization of the World

V.   Toward a Global Civilization?
    A.   Global Problems
    B.   Non-governmental Organizations
    C.   International Cooperation

Chapter Summary:

The Western world has seen amazing changes during the past thirty years. The most remarkable of these has been the disintegration of the Soviet Union, the release of its dependent countries, and the formation of a "new world order." As late as 1980 the Cold War was still being waged as an ideological struggle between Capitalism and Communism. However, by 1990 the entire picture had changed.

Beginning with Mikhail Gorbachev's attempt to reform the Soviet economy, pressure for change gathered such strength that the Soviet Union was dissolved and all the countries that were once a part of its sphere of influence were freed to go their own ways. Germany was reunited, while Yugoslavia crumbled into warring factions. Old enemies became friends in an effort to cope with threats of chaos from many sides, while ethnic groups once forcibly combined under single national banners began pulling apart to create autonomous states. The world about to enter the twenty-first century looked quite different from the one formed just after World War II.

While the "new world order" was just becoming evident, the challenges and problems facing it were already clear. Terrorism sponsored by dissident groups, tensions caused by the presence of alien residents in many countries, and threats to humankind from environmental abuses are the issues to occupy attention and energies for the foreseeable future. New trends in the arts, literature, the sciences, philosophy and religion reflect both the tensions of the Cold War now past and the uncertainties that come with its demise.

At present it is clear to all thoughtful people, that in order to cope with the dangers and realize the opportunities in our future we must begin to think globally. The nation-state, for so long the decisive institution in Western man's life, must take second place to the state of humankind if we are all to live full lives in peace with ourselves and the environment. The heroes of the future may be the men and women who show the way to think and live in this fashion.

Identify:

1.   "Evil empire" [p. 604]

2.   Mikhail Gorbachev [pp. 604, 607-609]

3.   *Perestroika* [p. 607]

4.   *Glasnost* [p. 607]

5.   Boris Yeltsin [p. 609]

6.   Solidarity [p. 609]

7.   Václav Havel [pp. 610-611]

8.   "Ethnic Cleansing" [p. 613]

9.   "Iron Lady" [pp. 615-616]

10.   François Mitterand [pp. 616-617]

11.   OPEC [p. 617]

12.   Green Movement [pp. 620-621]

13.   Pop Art [pp. 621-622]

14.   Samuel Beckett [p. 622]

15.   Albert Camus   [p. 622]

16.   E.F. Schumacher   [pp. 623-624]

Match the following words with their definitions:

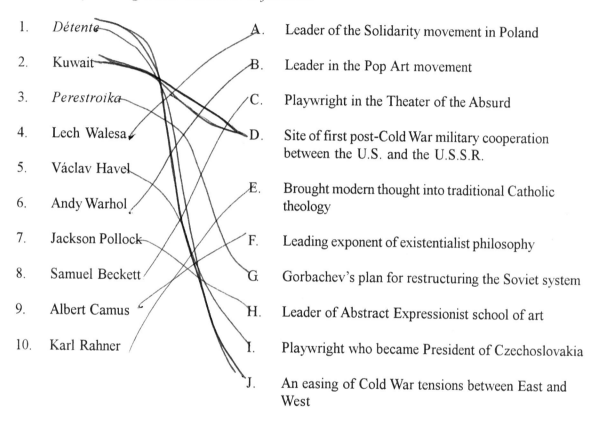

1.   *Détente*

2.   Kuwait

3.   *Perestroika*

4.   Lech Walesa

5.   Václav Havel

6.   Andy Warhol

7.   Jackson Pollock

8.   Samuel Beckett

9.   Albert Camus

10.   Karl Rahner

A.   Leader of the Solidarity movement in Poland

B.   Leader in the Pop Art movement

C.   Playwright in the Theater of the Absurd

D.   Site of first post-Cold War military cooperation between the U.S. and the U.S.S.R.

E.   Brought modern thought into traditional Catholic theology

F.   Leading exponent of existentialist philosophy

G.   Gorbachev's plan for restructuring the Soviet system

H.   Leader of Abstract Expressionist school of art

I.   Playwright who became President of Czechoslovakia

J.   An easing of Cold War tensions between East and West

Multiple-Choice:

1.   Mikhail Gorbachev's plan of *perestroika* at first aimed at a

   a.   market economy with complete free enterprise and homestead lands.
   b.   market economy with some free enterprise and some private property.
   c.   modified Marxism with the state controlling businesses.
   d.   return to pure Marxism, which he believed had been too quickly abandoned.

2.   Lech Walesa's Solidarity movement had the support of all the following *except*

    a.   the Communist Party.
    b.   the Catholic Church.
    c.   Polish intellectuals.
    d.   Polish workers.

3.   In Romania the move to overthrow the Communist regime in 1989 ended with Chairman Ceausescu being

    a.   exiled to Russia.
    b.   imprisoned for life.
    c.   demoted to farm workers.
    d.   tried and executed.

4.   With German reunification in 1990, the section that was formerly East Germany

    a.   became known as Middle Germany.
    b.   was the richest part of the new nation.
    c.   ceased to exist as a separate entity.
    d.   kept its own legislature and currency.

5.   After Tito's death in 1980, Yugoslavia was plunged into civil war by Serbians calling for

    a.   a restoration of the Catholic Faith in Bosnia.
    b.   new borders to accommodate Serb minorities.
    c.   repayment of loans made by the World Bank.
    d.   separate membership in NATO.

6.   The European Community remains today

    a.   too weak to affect world affairs.
    b.   limited to former NATO allies.
    c.   an organization dominated by Britain.
    d.   a purely economic and not a political union.

7.   In 1986 the Green Movement was strengthened when

    a.   a Green Party won the Italian national elections.
    b.   the EEC adopted a Green plan for handling industrial pollution.
    c.   a Soviet nuclear power plant exploded.
    d.   ten Nobel Prize winners endorsed its environmental proposals.

8.   Identify the *false* connection below.

   a.   Andy Warhol — Pop Art
   b.   Samuel Beckett — Theater of the Absurd
   c.   Jackson Pollock — Abstract Expressionism
   d.   Václav Havel — Serialist Music

9.   Jackson Pollock's art

   a.   represented a return to classical themes.
   b.   assaulted viewers with emotion and movement.
   c.   was too individualistic to have any influence on other artists.
   d.   led to laws banning pornography.

10.   Existentialism stressed

   a.   the need for people to create their own destiny.
   b.   a return to the God of traditional religion.
   c.   the human capacity to discover the one true purpose of the world.
   d.   a withdrawal from the active life.

Complete the following sentences:

1.   Because he considered the Soviet Union an _____ _____, U.S. President Ronald Reagan helped stimulate a new _____ _____.

2.   The new friendship between the U.S. and Russia was tested in 1990 when Iraq invaded _____, precipitating the _____ _____ War.

3.   Poland's move from Communist rule to a free market economy was led by the organization _____, a _____ movement directed by its president _____ _____.

4.   In the former Yugoslavia, the Serbian move to rid Bosnia of Muslims, called _____ cleansing, revived memories of _____ atrocities during World War II; yet NATO forces did not strongly retaliate until _____ Bosnians had been killed.

5.   At first greeted with euphoria, German reunification soon brought high _____. In the national elections of 1998, Helmut Kohl's Christian Democrats were defeated by the opposition _____ _____.

6.   Margaret Thatcher's government in Britain broke the power of the _____
_____ and attacked _____ with austerity measures, both
controversial, but her popularity soared with victory in the _____War.

8.   Women in the 1980s and 1990s formed _____ – _____ groups
to become more aware of male dominance over their lives. This led to new university
programs in _____ _____.

8.   Terrorist groups since 1970 have included the _____ _____ in
Italy, the _____ _____ Club in France, the
_____ – _____ gang in Germany, and the _____
_____ Army in Britain.

9.   "Theater of the Absurd" is best represented by Irishman _____
_____ and his play _____ _____ _____,
in which _____ happens.

10.   Existentialism holds that while the _____ of God is tragic, it liberates humans
from any preordained _____ and makes them depend only on
_____.

Place the following in chronological order and give dates:

1.   Helmut Kohl chosen Chancellor of West Germany   1.

2.   Dissolution of the U.S.S.R.   2.

3.   Francois Mitterand elected President of France   3.

4.   Reunification of Germany   4.

5.   Margaret Thatcher becomes British Prime Minister   5.

6.   Solidarity Movement emerges in Poland   6.

7.   Mikhail Gorbachev comes to power in the U.S.S.R.   7.

Questions for Critical Thought: In each essay, fully explore the topic by answering the questions that follow it.

1. The Fall of the Soviet Union. How did the Soviet system and its empire collapse? What role did Mikhail Gorbachev play in its demise? What was he trying to accomplish, and what actually happened? What directions did the Soviet states in Eastern Europe take? How does that part of the world look today?

2. The Democracies at the End of the Twentieth Century. What have been the major successes and failures of the democracies in the past quarter century? What leaders have made a difference, and in what directions have they led? What effect did the fall of the Soviet Union and the reunification of Germany have on the democracies?

3. The Contemporary Intellectual World. What have been the major trends in literature, art, philosophy, and religion in the last quarter century? What questions have they addressed? What innovations have they given the world? Where do they seem headed now?

4. The "New World Order" and Europe. What is Europe's role in the new world of the twentieth-first century? How has the demise of the Soviet Union affected this role? What has American military and cultural strength done to Europe? How did the Gulf War clarify Europe's role? How are the European countries coping with ethnic conflict and terrorism?

Analysis of Primary Source Documents:

1. What does Mikhail Gorbachev say made him decide a "restructuring" of the Soviet system was necessary? In what sense is restructuring needed in other countries?

2. Describe what Václav Havel calls the "contaminated moral environment." Who is to blame, and what is the solution? Is this analysis too profound or too simple? Explain.

3. What personal qualities come through in Margaret Thatcher's description of her entry into British politics? What obstacles did she face, and how did she meet them? What hints, if any, do you find that she will become the "Iron Lady" Prime Minister?

4. Explain E. F. Schumacher's argument that modern people are using their capital as if it were an income. Why does he say this practice is destructive? What is his solution? Will it work?

Map Exercise 17

Map Exercise 17:   The New Europe

Using various colors of pencil, shade and label the nations of the new Europe:

1.   Albania
2.   Austria
3.   Belarus
4.   Belgium
5.   Bosnia
6.   Bulgaria
7.   Croatia
8.   Czech Republic
9.   Estonia
10.   France
11.   Germany
12.   Greece
13.   Hungary
14.   Italy
15.   Kazakhstan
16.   Latvia
17.   Lithuania
18.   Netherlands
19.   Norway
20.   Portugal
21.   Romania
22.   Russia
23.   Slovakia
24.   Spain
25.   Sweden
26.   Switzerland
27.   Turkey
28.   United Kingdom
29.   Ukraine
30.   Yugoslavia

ANSWER KEY

CHAPTER 12

Matching

1. D
2. I
3. F
4. A
5. H
6. B
7. J
8. C
9. E
10. G

Multiple Choice

1. A
2. B
3. C
4. D
5. B
6. C
7. D
8. A
9. B
10. C

Completion

1. Medici, bank, alum
2. *Courtier*, aristocrat, prince
3. Ferrara, Mantua, library
4. diplomat, *The Prince*, moral
5. Petrarch, Cicero, Virgil
6. Leonardo, Michelangelo, Raphael
7. *The Last Supper*, inner life
8. *School of Athens*, balance, harmony, order
9. muscular, divine beauty
10. Julius II, Sixtus IV, Alexander VI

Chronology

1. End of Great Schism: 1417
2. Medici took power: 1434
3. Gutenberg Bible: 1455-6
4. Marriage of Ferdinand and Isabella: 1469
5. Bosworth Field: 1485
6. Expulsion of the Jews: 1492
7. First Medici pope: 1513

CHAPTER 13

Matching

1. D
2. F
3. A
4. J
5. C
6. B
7. H
8. I
9. E
10. G

Multiple Choice

1. A
2. D
3. B
4. A
5. D
6. C
7. A
8. C
9. B
10. D

Completion

1. *Folly*, corruptions, abuses
2. Augustinian, Ninety-five, indulgences
3. princes, peasants, state authority
4. Germany, Switzerland, Lord's Supper
5. adults, priest, minister
6. Catherine, Anne Boleyn, Edward VI
7. *Institutes*, sovereignty, predestination
8. wives, mothers, Eve
9. Ignatius, Loyola, soldiers, *Spiritual Exercises*
10. Council, Trent, Roman Inquisition

Chronology

1. Luther excommunicated: 1521
2. English Act of Supremacy: 1534
3. Calvin's *Institutes* published: 1536
4. Society of Jesus recognized: 1540
5. Council of Trent convenes: 1545
6. Peace of Augsburg: 1555
7. Death of Mary I: 1558

CHAPTER 14

Matching

1. E
2. C
3. I
4. H
5. G
6. F
7. J
8. B
9. D
10. A

Multiple Choice

1. D
2. B
3. B
4. D
5. D
6. A
7. A
8. B
9. B
10. A

Completion

1. Navigator, Vasco da Gama, de Albuquerqué
2. Hernando Cortés, Francesco Pizarro, *encomienda*
3. Huguenots, worship, public office
4. Supremacy, Elizabeth, Mary
5. armada, Catholic, Scotland, Ireland
6. Religious, German, Westphalia
7. El Greco, mannerist, Toledo
8. throne, doctors
9. Elizabeth, Lord Chamberlain's, Globe, Blackfriars
10. Don Quixote, Sancho Panza

Chronology

1. Diaz around Good Hope: 1487
2. Tordesillas: 1494
3. Netherlands: 1581
4. The Spanish Armada: 1588
5. Shakespeare in London: 1592
6. Edict of Nantes: 1598
7. Peace of Westphalia: 1648

CHAPTER 15

Matching

1. J
2. H
3. G
4. C
5. B
6. E
7. A
8. D
9. I
10. F

Multiple Choice

1. D
2. B
3. A
4. B
5. A
6. D
7. A
8. A
9. C
10. D

Completion

1. Nantes, Fontainebleau
2. finances, mercantilism, export, import
3. reform decrees, aristocrats
4. Frederick William, army, commissariat
5. Western, backward, mercantilist, Holy Synod
6. Oliver Cromwell, Parliament, governor
7. Catholic, Orange, Mary
8. constitutional, law, rights
9. commerce, Rembrandt
10. *Misanthrope*, clergy

Chronology

1. Execution of Charles I: 1649
2. *Leviathan*: 1651
3. Turkish siege of Vienna: 1683
4. Edict of Fontainebleau: 1685
5. England's Glorious Revolution: 1688
6. Peter Romanov's trip to the West: 1697-98
7. Frederick III becomes Frederick I: 1701

CHAPTER 16

Matching

1. H
2. A
3. J
4. G
5. D
6. B
7. F
8. C
9. I
10. E

Multiple Choice

1. D
2. A
3. B
4. D
5. A
6. B
7. A
8. A
9. D
10. C

Completion

1. Aristotle, Galen, nature, anatomy
2. Geometrizes, mathematical, Hermetic
3. geocentric, heliocentric, complicated
4. mountains, moons, sun
5. machine, absolute, gravitation
6. liver, veins, arteries
7. astronomy, Berlin Academy, woman
8. mind, material world, Dualism
9. Science, Christian, *Pensées*
10. experiments, observations, inductive

Chronology

1. Copernicus' *Revolutions*: 1543
2. Galileo's *Messenger*: 1610
3. Bacon's *Instauration*: 1626
4. Harvey's *Motion*: 1628
5. Descartes' *Method*: 1637
6. Pascal's *Pensées*: 1662
7. Newton's *Principia*: 1686

CHAPTER 17

Matching

1. E
2. D
3. I
4. H
5. G
6. A
7. B
8. J
9. C
10. F

Multiple Choice

1. B
2. A
3. D
4. C
5. C
6. C
7. A
8. B
9. B
10. C

Completion

1. lady, lover, mechanistic universe
2. Catholic Church, monarchy, checks, balances
3. Deism, Mechanic, crush
4. *Encyclopedia*, superstition, tolerance
5. Mercantilism, passive policeman
6. *Social Contract*, *Emile*, private property
7. Aristocratic, Vierzehnheiligen
8. *St. Matthew's*, *Messiah*, *Giovanni*
9. carnival, sexual, consumption
10. deterrents, brutality, capital punishment

Chronology

1. Locke's *Essay*: 1690
2. Montesquieu's *Persian Letters*: 1721
3. Diderot's *Encyclopedia* begun: 1751
4. Rousseau's *Social Contract*: 1762
5. Voltaire's *Treatise*: 1763
6. Smith's *Wealth of Nations*: 1776
7. Wollstonecraft's *Vindication*: 1792

CHAPTER 18

Matching

1. D
2. I
3. J
4. G
5. A
6. B
7. E
8. C
9. F
10. H

Multiple Choice

1. D
2. D
3. B
4. D
5. C
6. A
7. D
8. C
9. C
10. A

Completion

1. pocket, landed
2. George III, French, Napoleon
3. speech, press, toleration
4. Maria Theresa, philosophy
5. Emelyan Pugachev, executed, rural
6. woman, Silesia, Austrian Succession
7. India, North America, empire
8. Abraham, Wolfe, Montcalm, Britain
9. textiles, guild workshops, cottage industries
10. cotton, coffee, sugar, slave

Chronology

1. Hanoverian succession: 1714
2. Frederick the Great begins reign: 1740
3. Seven Years' War: 1756-63
4. Pugachev Rebellion: 1773-5
5. Joseph II begins sole rule: 1780
6. Pitt the Younger: 1783
7. Third Partition of Poland: 1795

CHAPTER 19

Matching

1. D
2. J
3. A
4. G
5. B
6. H
7. C
8. F
9. I
10. E

Multiple Choice

1. A
2. D
3. B
4. C
5. B
6. D
7. B
8. C
9. C
10. B

Completion

1. Stamp Act, Second
2. natural rights, Enlightenment
3. finances, Versailles, Revolution
4. people, state, civil constitution
5. internal enemies, guillotine, Terror
6. Saint, Notre Dame, marry
7. Virtue, Thermidor, Directory
8. processions, seminaries, enemy
9. Britain, wage war, hegemony
10. Elba, Waterloo, St. Helena

Chronology

1. Seven Years' War ends: 1763
2. Declaration of American Independence: 1776
3. Storming of the Bastille: 1789
4. Louis XVI executed: 1793
5. Continental System: 1806
6. Russian fiasco: 1812
7. Battle of Waterloo: 1815

CHAPTER 20

Matching

1. D
2. E
3. H
4. A
5. F
6. C
7. G
8. B
9. I
10. J

Multiple Choice

1. D
2. B
3. D
4. B
5. B
6. D
7. A
8. B
9. C
10. B

Completion

1. coal, iron, rivers, size
2. Hargreaves, Cartwright
3. locomotive, *Rocket*
4. Crystal Palace, Kensington, Britain
5. technical, inventors, factories
6. Catholic, Protestant, potato
7. Poor Law, atmospheric, sanitation
8. size, broken, cheap
9. democracy, male, payment
10. eight, ten, mines

Chronology

1. Watt's rotary steam engine: 1782
2. Cartwright's power loom: 1787
3. Trevithick's steam locomotive: 1804
4. Luddite Attack: 1812
5. People's Charter: 1838
6. Ten Hours Act: 1847
7. Great Exhibition: 1851

CHAPTER 21

Matching

1. D
2. H
3. A
4. J
5. F
6. B
7. I
8. C
9. G
10. E

Multiple Choice

1. B
2. C
3. C
4. D
5. D
6. D
7. C
8. A
9. B
10. A

Completion

1. Metternich, legitimacy, Bourbons
2. Simón Bolívar, José de San Martín
3. Russia, France, Britain, independent
4. military revolt, secret police
5. *On Liberty*, liberty, individual
6. Cotton, New Lanark, New Harmony
7. Bourgeois, Dutch
8. Louis-Philippe, Charles Louis Napoleon Bonaparte
9. Young Italy, Charles Albert, Austrians, Lombardy
10. Goethe, Walter Scott, Mary Shelley

Chronology

1. *Reflections* written: 1790
2. Wars of Independence in Latin America begin: 1819
3. Greek revolt against the Turks begins: 1821
4. Nicholas I: 1825
5. July Revolution in France: 1830
6. British Reform Act: 1832
7. Revolts or revolutions in France, Germany, Italy, and Austria: 1848

CHAPTER 22

Matching

1. E
2. H
3. C
4. A
5. J
6. D
7. I
8. F
9. B
10. G

Multiple Choice

1. A
2. D
3. C
4. D
5. A
6. B
7. A
8. D
9. B
10. C

Completion

1. Ottoman, Crimean, Britain, concert
2. Italian patriot, Victor Emmanuel, Savoy
3. Denmark, Austria, France, Empire
4. property, marry, assassination
5. Disraeli, Liberal
6. American, Dominion, foreign affairs
7. *Communist Manifesto*, proletariat, bourgeoisie, classless
8. plants, animals, *Man*, animal
9. romantic, adultery, suicide
10. angels, goddesses, ugliness

Chronology

1. Second French Empire proclaimed: 1852
2. Russian Emancipation Edict: 1861
3. American Civil War ends: 1865
4. Austro-Prussian War: 1866
5. British Reform Act: 1867
6. Italy annexes Rome: 1870
7. German Empire proclaimed: 1871

CHAPTER 23

Matching

1. A
2. I
3. F
4. E
5. C
6. H
7. B
8. J
9. D
10. G

Multiple Choice

1. C
2. A
3. C
4. B
5. A
6. D
7. C
8. A
9. C
10. D

Completion

1. industrial, agricultural, polarization
2. white collar, teaching, nursing
3. revolution, evolution, gradualist
4. 960,000; 6,500,000; 172,000; 2,700,000
5. London, Liverpool, private enterprise
6. Condoms, diaphragms, World War
7. political, patriotism, language
8. commune, shot, penal colony
9. Prussian, monarchy, aristocracy, emperor
10. constitutional monarchy, social reform, martial law

Chronology

1. Thomas Cook's first tour: 1841
2. Paris Commune: 1871
3. Public Health Act: 1875
4. Bismarck's anti-socialist law: 1878
5. First birth control clinic: 1882
6. Reform Act: 1884
7. First human flight: 1903

CHAPTER 24

Matching

1. G
2. I
3. D
4. F
5. E
6. H
7. A
8. J
9. B
10. C

Multiple Choice

1. A
2. C
3. A
4. A
5. D
6. C
7. B
8. C
9. C
10. A

Completion

1. quanta, atoms, Newton
2. relativity, observer, time, space
3. unconscious, oblivious, dreams
4. Darwinism, biological necessity, father
5. property, capitalism, socialism, Marxism
6. light, vision, delicate
7. Asia, Africa, scramble
8. Transvaal, Orange Free State, British
9. Commonwealth, Australia, New Zealand
10. Balkans, Bosnia, Herzegovina

Chronology

1. British take Hong Kong: 1842
2. Suez Canal opened: 1869
3. Victoria crowned Empress of India: 1876
4. First Zionist Congress: 1897
5. Russo-Japanese War: 1905
6. Triple Entente formed: 1907
7. Japan annexes Korea: 1910

CHAPTER 25

Matching

1. J
2. D
3. G
4. A
5. I
6. B
7. E
8. C
9. H
10. F

Multiple Choice

1. A
2. B
3. A
4. B
5. A
6. D
7. A
8. B
9. D
10. B

Completion

1. Irish, Poles, Slavs
2. Bosnian, Serbian, Black Hand
3. Paris, Marne, trench
4. Lawrence, Ottoman
5. *Lusitania*, submarine warfare
6. dissenters, censored, suspended
7. provisional government, abdicate
8. Bolsheviks, Lenin, Brest-Litovsk
9. Fourteen Points, Britain, France
10. demilitarize, reparations, Rhineland

Chronology

1. Francis Ferdinand assassinated: June 28, 1914
2. World War I begins: August 1, 1914
3. Battle of Gallipoli begins: April 25, 1915
4. U.S. enters the war: April 6, 1917
5. Treaty of Brest-Litovsk: March 3, 1918
6. Armistice: November 11, 1918
7. Paris Conference begins: January 18, 1919

CHAPTER 26

Matching

1. G
2. I
3. B
4. A
5. J
6. C
7. H
8. D
9. E
10. F

Multiple Choice

1. C
2. B
3. C
4. D
5. B
6. B
7. B
8. A
9. D
10. D

Completion

1. League, Nations, France, Germany
2. Reparations, Ruhr, inflation
3. demand, public works, deficit spending
4. working, New Deal
5. Socialist, Fascist, *Il Duce*
6. Jews, Heinrich Himmler, Hitler Youth
7. Bolsheviks, Leon Trotsky, industrialize, collectivize
8. *Kraft durch Freude*
9. Purposelessness, Unconscious, ornamentation
10. *Ulysses*, consciousness, Dublin

Chronology

1. Death of Lenin: 1924
2. Fascist dictatorship established in Italy: 1925
3. National Government begins in Britain: 1931
4. Franklin Roosevelt elected: 1932
5. Hitler dictatorship begins in Germany: 1934
6. Popular Front formed in France: 1936
7. *Kristallnacht* in Germany: 1938

CHAPTER 27

Matching

1. J
2. D
3. B
4. F
5. H
6. A
7. I
8. C
9. G
10. E

Multiple Choice

1. B
2. C
3. A
4. A
5. A
6. C
7. A
8. D
9. C
10. D

Completion

1. Rhineland, Austria, Czechoslovakia
2. appeasement, peace, times
3. Poland, *blitzkrieg*, France
4. Pétain, Vichy
5. Pearl Harbor, Co-prosperity Sphere
6. North Africa, Stalingrad, Coral Sea
7. Invasion, Hiroshima, Nagasaki
8. Madagascar, Reinhard Heydrich, annihilation
9. Russia, Night Witches
10. spheres, influence, self-determination

Chronology

1. German occupation of Rhineland: March 7, 1936
2. German invasion of Poland: September 1, 1939
3. Battle of Britain: Fall, 1940
4. Japanese attack Pearl Harbor: December 7, 1941
5. German surrender at Stalingrad: February 2, 1943
6. Allied invasion of France: June 6, 1944
7. Atomic bomb dropped on Hiroshima: August 6, 1945

CHAPTER 28

Matching

1. D
2. I
3. G
4. A
5. C
6. B
7. E
8. J
9. F
10. H

Multiple Choice

1. A
2. D
3. C
4. B
5. C
6. A
7. C
8. A
9. B
10. B

Completion

1. British, Greece, Turkey
2. Soviet, *Foreign Affairs*, containment
3. missiles, blockade, invade
4. Philippines, India, Indochina
5. First World, Second World, Third World
6. Eastern Europe, Hungary, Czechoslovakia
7. NATO, nuclear, automobiles, armaments
8. economic miracle, Konrad Adenauer
9. Bank, Insurance, Health
10. homosexuality, education, birth control

Chronology

1. Truman Doctrine: 1947
2. Formation of NATO: 1949
3. Formation of the Warsaw Pact: 1955
4. De Gaulle assumes power: 1958
5. Erection of Berlin Wall: 1961
6. Cuban Missile Crisis: 1962
7. Prague Spring: 1968

CHAPTER 29

Matching

1. J
2. D
3. G
4. A
5. I
6. B
7. H
8. C
9. F
10. E

Multiple Choice

1. B
2. A
3. D
4. C
5. B
6. D
7. C
8. D
9. B
10. A

Completion

1. evil empire, arms race
2. Kuwait, Persian Gulf
3. Solidarity, labor, Lech Walesa
4. ethnic, Nazi, 250,000
5. unemployment, Social Democrats
6. labor unions, inflation, Falklands
7. consciousness-raising, Women's Studies
8. Red Brigades, Charles Martel, Baader-Meinhof, Irish Republican
9. Samuel Beckett, *Waiting for Godot,* nothing
10. death, destiny, themselves

Chronology

1. Thatcher becomes British Prime Minister: 1979
2. Solidarity Movement emerges in Poland: 1980
3. Mitterand elected President of France: 1981
4. Kohl chosen Chancellor of West Germany: 1982
5. Gorbachev comes to power in U.S.S.R.: 1985
6. Reunification of Germany: 1990
7. Dissolution of U.S.S.R.: 1991